TEN CONTEMPORARY POETS

HARRAP'S ENGLISH CLASSICS

COMUS AND SOME SHORTER POEMS OF MILTON
Edited by E. M. W. TILLYARD, Litt.D., F.B.A., formerly Master of Jesus College, Cambridge
and PHYLLIS B. TILLYARD, M.A., Girton College, Cambridge

MILTON: PARADISE LOST: BOOKS I AND II
Edited by E. M. W. TILLYARD, Litt.D., F.B.A., formerly Master of Jesus College, Cambridge
and PHYLLIS B. TILLYARD, M.A., Girton College, Cambridge

MILTON: PARADISE LOST: BOOKS IX AND X
Edited by E. M. W. TILLYARD, Litt.D., F.B.A., formerly Master of Jesus College, Cambridge

CHAUCER: THE PROLOGUE TO THE CANTERBURY TALES
Edited by R. T. DAVIES, M.A., Lecturer in English, Liverpool University

CHAUCER: THE KNIGHT'S TALE
Edited by J. A. W. BENNETT, M.A., D.Phil., Professor of Mediæval and Renaissance English
in the University of Cambridge

CHAUCER: THE PARDONER'S TALE
Edited by NEVILL COGHILL, M.A., Merton Professor of English Literature in the University of
Oxford, *and* CHRISTOPHER TOLKIEN, M.A., Fellow of New College, Oxford

CHAUCER: THE NUN'S PRIEST'S TALE
Edited by NEVILL COGHILL, M.A., Merton Professor of English Literature in the University of
Oxford, *and* CHRISTOPHER TOLKIEN, M.A., Fellow of New College, Oxford

TWENTIETH-CENTURY NARRATIVE POEMS
Compiled and edited by MAURICE WOLLMAN, M.A.

TEN TWENTIETH-CENTURY POETS
Edited by MAURICE WOLLMAN, M.A.

A BOOK OF MODERN PROSE
Edited by DOUGLAS BROWN, M.A., formerly of The Perse School, Cambridge

TWENTIETH-CENTURY SHORT STORIES
Edited by DOUGLAS R. BARNES, Senior English Master, Minchenden School, Southgate,
and R. F. EGFORD, Senior English Master, Selhurst Grammar School

NINE TWENTIETH-CENTURY ESSAYISTS
Edited by HAROLD GARDINER, Senior English Master, Bedales School

SELECTED POEMS OF WILLIAM WORDSWORTH
Edited by DONALD DAVIE, Ph.D., Fellow of Gonville and Caius College, Cambridge

TEN CONTEMPORARY POETS
Compiled and edited by MAURICE WOLLMAN, M.A.

Ten Contemporary Poets

Compiled and edited by
MAURICE WOLLMAN, M.A.

GEORGE G. HARRAP & CO. LTD
London Toronto Wellington Sydney

OTHER BOOKS EDITED BY
MAURICE WOLLMAN

Twentieth-century Narrative Poems
Ten Twentieth-century Poets
Seven Themes in Modern Verse
The Harrap Book of Modern Verse (with Kathleen B. Parker)
Harrap's Junior Book of Modern Verse (with Dorothy M. Hurst)
Happenings (with David Grugeon)
Modern Poems for the Commonwealth (with John Spencer)

First published in Great Britain 1963
by GEORGE G. HARRAP & CO. LTD
182 High Holborn, London, W.C.1

Reprinted: 1966, 1968

This edition © *George G. Harrap & Co. Ltd* 1963

Composed in Monotype Bembo and printed by
Butler & Tanner Ltd, Frome and London
Made in Great Britain

PREFACE

THESE ten poets are contemporary in that they face the forces and values of life today and make poetry from them. Facing these standards does not mean that they necessarily accept them; doubt or despair may arise. Poets have always been questioners, and poetry has always asked questions. The poet today confronts the present, and accepts here, rejects there, and questions everywhere. Some of these questions have been the source of poems ever since Greek times; some of these questions are peculiarly twentieth-century questions leading to twentieth-century poems. But all the questions are fundamental to present-day life, and the poet sees deeply and prophetically into the implications of many present-day phenomena. His themes are the permanent and continuing relations of human life, threatened by the speed of present history and technology. He often does not answer his own questions; but the mere propounding of the question is valuable in itself. Acceptance or (implied) rejection may follow questioning, but the question itself is the important thing.

The brief introduction to each section of the anthology attempts to give a general view of the poet's work but with special relevance to the selection that follows and sometimes to one particular poem, which is considered typical of the poet and which is discussed at some slight length. The ideas put forward in these introductions are condensed and are intended as sign-posts for the teacher, commenting and adding as he goes, rather than dogmatic assertions for the student to learn and accept without question. Many of the ideas are capable of expansion and of illustration from the poems that follow.

ACKNOWLEDGMENTS

THANKS are due to the following for kind permission to print the poems included in this Anthology:

Thomas Blackburn, for MS poems, and Messrs Putnam and Co., Ltd, for poems from *The Next Word* and *A Smell of Burning*, and *The Poetry Review* for 'En Route'; D. J. Enright and Messrs Routledge and Kegan Paul, Ltd, for poems from *The Laughing Hyena*, and Messrs Secker and Warburg, Ltd, for poems from *Bread Rather than Blossoms*, and Messrs Chatto and Windus, Ltd, for poems from *Some Men Are Brothers* and *Addictions*; Robert Graves and International Authors N.V., for poems from *Collected Poems* 1959 and 'The Simpleton' and 'Here Live Your Life Out!' from *More Poems*, both published by Messrs Cassell and Co., Ltd; Thom Gunn and Messrs Faber and Faber, Ltd, for poems from *Fighting Terms*, *The Sense of Movement*, and *My Sad Captains*; Ted Hughes and Messrs Faber and Faber, Ltd, for poems from *The Hawk in the Rain*, *Lupercal*, and *Meet My Folks*; Patrick Kavanagh, for MS poems, and for 'Primrose', from *A Soul for Sale*, and Messrs Longmans, Green and Co., Ltd, for poems from *Come Dance with Kitty Stobling*; Louis MacNeice and Messrs Faber and Faber, Ltd, for poems from *Collected Poems*, *Ten Burnt Offerings*, *Visitations*, and *Solstices*; Vernon Scannell, for poems from *A Mortal Pitch*, and Messrs Putnam and Co., Ltd, for poems from *The Masks of Love* and *A Sense of Danger*, and *The Poetry Review* for 'A City Remembered', and *The Times Literary Supplement* for 'Makers and Creatures'; Hal Summers, for MS poems, and poems from *Smoke after Flame* and *Hinterland*; R. S. Thomas and Messrs Rupert Hart-Davis, Ltd, for poems from *Song at the Year's Turning*, *Poetry for Supper* and *Tares*.

INDEX OF AUTHORS

    *

THOMAS BLACKBURN

❦

BORN in Cumberland, 1916. Educated Bromsgrove School and Durham University. Held the Gregory Poetry Fellowship at Leeds University for two years. Lecturer in English at the College of St Mark and St John, Chelsea. Works include: *The Outer Darkness* (1953); *The Holy Stone* (1954); *In the Fire* (1956); *The Next Word* (1958); *45-60* (1961)—an anthology; *A Smell of Burning* (1961); *The Price of an Eye* (1961)—literary criticism; *A Breathing Space* (1964).

Thomas Blackburn's concern in his poetry is with the deepest and most significant of human experiences—the relationship of people in childhood and in marriage, the loss of identity in love and the gaining of a new identity, the conflict in oneself between various forces, and the give and take of everyday life. As he wrote in the preface to his Anthology of post-war poetry, 'Poems are often concerned with the struggle to understand the complexities of ourselves. . . . They try to make articulate what one might call the growing pains of life.' His analysis of human feelings, especially his own, is detached and exact, sometimes sardonic and occasionally self-mocking. Much of his verse is cast in the form of a myth or a classical allusion, which is shown to have relevance to today. The Fates are in man's heart, and his first business is to defeat them or exorcize them or placate them or escape from them. While the influence of the later Yeats is to be seen in this use of myth and in the bare rhetorical style, the first poem here has an Auden-like theme and beginning—the idea that by putting examples of primitive savagery, superstitions, and magic in museums we cannot shut them off. His language is forceful and colloquial, searching and persuasive.

The Lucky Marriage begins with a light-hearted enquiry into the meaning of those fairy-tales in which Cinderella marries the prince or the kitchen-boy marries the princess. Gradually, by a scarcely perceptible transition, the poem moves into a darker realm, and considers the nature of sexual passion, the problem of human identity, the rôle of suffering and rejection in the growth of spiritual insight. The poet's ability to sustain a melodic flow ensures that the reader shall respond to and understand the argument without stumbling over its complexities.

The Citizens: A Chorus from a Play

After the marsh was drained and its vast monsters
Had gasped their lives out in the well-rinsed air,
Our city corporation cleaned the fosse up
And charged us sixpence to see Grendell's lair.
We thought that with the Great Panjandrum banished
An era of sweet dreams was sure to start;
But gracious no, only his cave has vanished;
Don't look now, but he's walking in your heart.

After Sir Hercules had combed the mountains
And killed the Nemean lion, our woods were bare.
On feast days now we can go out to picnic
And if it rains take shelter in its lair;
The pebbles and the moss are quite enchanting.
I think I hear the ancient roaring start.
What's that you say? I said the ancient roaring,
Excuse me but it's coming from your heart.

Upon our museum shelves we keep the omens
That after school before they go to bed
Children may see some curious time-worn bauble
A pickled toad, a stone, a Gorgon's head.
Why do they cry in sleep, the silly children,
Of birds that speak, of snakes that hiss and dart

Upon a woman's scalp? Put them to silence.
You cannot stop the language of the heart.

In days gone by the warriors would sit feasting,
Then freeze to silence at the slow footfall
Of Grendell's furious dam who rocked the postern,
Then strode through snapping beams into the hall.
That monster comes no more by field or river,
But still our dwelling-place is torn apart
By human hands—like mine—our children ravaged;
Oh, hide me from the fury of the heart.

An Invitation

Holding with shaking hands a letter from some
Official—high up he says in his Ministry,
I note that I am invited to Birmingham,
There pedagogues to address for a decent fee.
'We like to meet,' he goes on, 'men eminent
In the field of letters each year,' and that's well put,
Though I find his words not wholly relevant
To this red-eyed fellow whose mouth tastes rank as soot.
No doubt what he's thinking of is poetry
When 'Thomas Blackburn' he writes, and not the fuss
A life makes when it has no symmetry,
Though the term 'a poet' being mainly posthumous,
Since I'm no stiff, is inappropriate.
What I can confirm is the struggle that never lets up
Between the horses of Plato beneath my yoke,

One after Light, and for Hell not giving a rap,
The other only keen on infernal smoke.
And poems...? From time to time they commemorate
Some particularly dirty battle between these two;
I put the letter down—what's the right note?
'Dear Sir,' I type, 'how nice to speak to you!'

An Epitaph

By much speaking I fled from silence,
To many friends from the one stranger,
By food and drink I cheated hunger,
And by meek words, abuse and violence.

My loss increased as I grew richer,
My load more great with lighter burden,
With less guilt, more sought I pardon.
As light flowered, I grew blinder.

I quenched my thirst by lack of water,
And found myself where I was absent,
Faith half I proved by the inconstant
Moon: truth because I was a liar.

Now far still from the heart's centre,
But with less storm, less crying,
I wait for birth again, now dying
Has opened its door and let me enter.

En Route

It's strange, I thought, though half now stretches
Behind my back, how this road clutches
To its small grit and measuring stone,
Still more of life as I walk on;
Must all directions be subdued
By the compulsion of the road?

And strange it is, since there're no fences,
I do not take the path which glances
Aside from this, as if one strict
Intention gathered up all fact;
Is it because I'm whittled down
To the sharp stones I journey on?

Once certainly the traveller hurried
Down every path the wind unburied.
Finding, however, each new search
Swung back to the old line of march,
And that through detours I could not
Bye-pass myself or the road's grit.

Though still a side-lane light discloses,
I would hold back from its green mazes,
Sensing, though light it may reflect,
Once entered it would be blunt fact,
And so a double tax be owed
To the compulsion of the road.

Not that today they do not differ,
Myself, and the relentless pressure
Of gravel underneath my feet,
But now I glimpse I half beget,
Step after step, what I walk on,
And know I am the origin

Of so much love and hate which gathers
Round those who with me are wayfarers.
Perhaps when to myself, the dreamer,
I wake and understand the ardour
In which all burn, more clear I'll know
Who others are, myself also,

Than when it seemed far off, the fever
Which shakes me now. Since doom and glamour
No man can fly from or possess,
By stillness I make good their loss,
And find, upon the edge of winter,
More plain the way as light grows fainter.

Last night I dreamt the road diminished
To a last stone, and where it perished
I met a child beside a river,
Who asked if I would bear him over.
I knelt then as if asking pardon,
But on my back his little burden

Than the whole world became much greater,
As stepping down into the water
I braced myself to find what could
Sustain my feet when I was dead

And at long last no debt was owed,
Since on my shoulders lay the road.

Hospital for Defectives

By your unnumbered charities
A miracle disclose,
Lord of the Images, whose love
The eyelid and the rose
Takes for a language, and today
Tell to me what is said
By these men in a turnip field
And their unleavened bread.

For all things seem to figure out
The stirrings of your heart,
And two men pick the turnips up
And two men pull the cart;
And yet between the four of them
No word is ever said
Because the yeast was not put in
Which makes the human bread.
But three men stare on vacancy
And one man strokes his knees;
What is the meaning to be found
In such dark vowels as these?

Lord of the Images, whose love
The eyelid and the rose

Takes for a metaphor, today,
Beneath the warder's blows,
The unleavened man did not cry out
Or turn his face away;
Through such men in a turnip field
What is it that you say?

Footnote for a Painting by Arthur Boid

Certainly we affirm this as a truth
Though the statement it makes is hard to assess
In terms other than itself. It has no breath,
This picture, nothing that one can diagnose.—
But look—that only is appropriate—
How the lovers for a moment coalesce
In a myth, in an immensity of landscape,
Desperate, but not, since this is human, without hope.
It is their blackness elates and terrifies,
Since by opposing some dimension quite other
To that which custom gentles and dries,
It reminds us of what in fact we always are.
Human, I mean, and so reaching for no
Conclusion that it is possible to interpret
With a brain; like this picture, which can only say
What it is and that other statements are not
Relevant. What matters is the particular
Instant, consumed, as it always is, in unwithering fire.

Café Talk

'Of course,' I said, 'we cannot hope to find
What we are looking for in anyone;
They glitter, maybe, but are not the sun,
This pebble here, that bit of apple-rind.
Still, it's the Alpine sun that makes them burn,
And what we're looking for, some indirect
Glint of itself each of us may reflect,
And so shed light about us as we turn.'
Sideways she looked and said, 'How you go on!'
And was the stone and rind, their shinings gone.

'It is some hard dry scale we must break through,
A deadness round the life. I cannot make
That pebble shine. Its clarity must take
Sunlight into itself and prove it true.
It is our childishness that clutters up
With scales out of the past a present speech,
So that the sun's white finger cannot reach
An adult prism.'
              'Will they never stop,
Your words?' she said and settled to the dark.

'But we use words, we cannot grunt or bark,
Use any surer means to make that first
Sharp glare of origin again appear
Through the marred glass,' I cried, 'but can you hear?'
'Quite well, you needn't shout.' I felt the thirst
Coil back into my body till it shook,

And, 'Are you cold?' she said, then ceased to look
And picked a bit of cotton from her dress.
Out in the square a child began to cry,
What was not said buzzed round us like a fly.

I knew quite well that silence was my cue,
But jabbered out, 'This meeting place we need,
If we can't find it, still desire may feed
And strengthen on the acts it cannot do.
By suffered depredations we may grow
To bear our energies just strong enough,
And at the last through perdurable stuff
A little of their radiance may show:
If we keep still.' Then she, 'It's getting late.'
A waiter came and took away a plate.

Then from the darkness an accordion;
'These pauses, love, perhaps in them, made free,
Life slips out of its gross machinery,
And turns upon itself in unison.'
It was quite dark now you must understand
And something of a red mouth on a wall
Joined with the music and the alcohol
And pushed me to the fingers of her hand.
Well, there it was, itself and quite complete,
Accountable, small bones there were and meat.

It did not press on mine or shrink away,
And, since no outgone need can long invest
Oblivion with a living interest,
I drew back and had no more words to say.
Outside the streets were like us and quite dead.

Yet anything more suited to my will,
I can't imagine, than our very still
Return to no place; as the darkness shed
Increasing whiteness on the far icefall,
A growth of light there was; and that is all.

The Lucky Marriage

I often wonder as the fairy-story
Tells how the little goose-girl found her prince,
Or of the widowed queen who stopped her carriage
And threw a rose down to the gangling dunce,
What is the meaning of this lucky marriage
Which lasts forever, it is often said,
Because I know too well such consummation
Is not a question of a double bed,
Or of the wedding bells and royal procession
With twenty major-domos at its head.

At least its bride and groom must be rejected,
The fairy godmother will only call
On Cinders scrubbing tiles beside the chimney
While her proud sisters foot it at the ball;
From all but the last son without a birthright
The beggarwoman hoards her magic seed.
Well, if they'd had the good luck of their siblings
And found occasion kinder to their need,
They would have spent their breath on natural
    pleasures

And had no time for murmurs in the night:
They heard because they were condemned to silence,
And learnt to see because they had no light.

I mean the elder son and cherished sister
Know but the surface of each common day;
It takes the cunning eye of the rejected
To dip beneath that skin of shadow-play
And come into the meaning of a landscape.
I think that every bird and casual stone
Are syllables thrust down from some broad language
That we must ravel out and make our own.
Yet who is ever turned towards that journey
Till deprivations riddle through the heart?
And so I praise the goose-girl and the scullion
Beside a midden or a refuse cart.

And yet all images for this completion
Somehow bye-pass its real ghostliness
Which can't be measured by a sweating finger,
Or any salt and carnal nakedness.
Although two heads upon a single pillow
May be the metaphor that serves it best,
No lying down within a single moment
Will give the outward going any rest;
It's only when we reach beyond our pronouns
And come into ourselves that we are blest.
Is this the meaning of the lucky marriage
Which lasts forever, it is often said,
Between the goose-girl and the kitchen servant,
Who have no wedding ring or mutual bed?

A Small Keen Wind

My wife, for six months now in sinister
Tones, has muttered incessantly about divorce,
And since of the woman I'm fond, this dark chatter
Is painful as well as a bit monotonous.
But marvel one must, when she fishes out of that trunk
Like rags, my shadier deeds for all to see,
With, 'This you did when sober, and that when drunk!'
The remarkable powers of human memory.
For although I wriggle like mad when she whistles up
Some particularly nasty bit of handiwork
From my past, the dirty linen I cannot drop
Since 'Thomas Blackburn' is stitched by the laundry mark.
So I gather the things and say, 'Yes, these are mine,
Though some cleaner items are not upon your list,'
Then walk with my bundle of rags to another room,
Since I will not play the role of delinquent ghost
And be folded up by guilt in the crook of an arm.
I saw tonight—walking to cool the mind—
A little moonshine on a garden wall,
And, as I brooded, felt a small keen wind
Stroll from the Arctic at its own sweet will.

A Smell of Burning

After each savage, hysterical episode,
So common with us, my mother would sniff the air

And murmur, 'Nurse, would you look at the upstairs fire,
I smell burning, something's alight somewhere.'
But a red coal never was found, or jet of gas,
Scorching dry board, or paint-work beginning to melt;
And too young was I in that nursery time to guess
What smoking, subjective fire she really smelt.
Nowadays I know quite well from hers they came,
And my father's mouth, when the hot tongues crackled
    and spat;
But what mattered then was a trick of dodging flame,
And keeping some breath alive in the heat of it.
I have it still that inbred dodging trick;
But always—when fire beset—I see them turning,
My parents, to name elsewhere their sour fire reek,
And touch myself and know what's really burning.

For a Child

And have I put upon your shoulders then,
What in myself I have refused to bear,
My own and the confusion of dead men,
You of all these, my daughter, made my heir,
The furies and the griefs of which I stayed
Quite unaware?

Perhaps because I did not with my tongue
State these sharp energies into the mind,
They are the shadows you grow up among;
You suffer darkness because I was blind,

Take up the chaosses that in myself
Were unconfined.

If I should say, I also know the tart
Flavour of other men, as my excuse,
And took into myself their broken heart,
That's not the point, abuse remains abuse;
May chaos though have light within your mind,
And be of use.

Number Unobtainable

Though forty years' nostalgia should have brought
One fact home, *She* is not upon the line,
Even to my rawness and distempered thought,
How self-engendered is this zest of mine,
Now, as the telephone rasps out her absence,
From kennels of the sea they reawaken,
Poseidon's dogs, and bald and middle-aged
By their first leap and outcry I am shaken.

Trewarmett

Darkness, feathers are shed;
These birds are gathered back
By the enormous hand
That cast them at dawn seaward

In crumbs of living bread
To their forefathering rock.

Piercing the lense of a wave,
From the beat of it and the swell
The feathered life they have
Is indivisible,
As from the undertow
And skin of a nervous sea
Fish and themselves also
They reap perpetually.
Being clothed and without a seam
In the pouring waters they thread,
How can they miss their aim,
By the loose surge targetted
Forever towards their home.

Darkness, feathers are shed;
From this bird-whitened stone
I watch a cormorant pluck
Life from the nervous sea,
With a moon behind my back,
Conscious of God knows what
Anxious irrelevance,
As these birds swim in the eye
Of the green circumstance
From which I am undone
By my duplicity.

Watching a bird, and a man
Watching a bird in the surf,
Watched by a man, and that faint

Rim of horizon far off
Where darkness breeds from a glint
Of metal, I wait for the tide
To work its equation out.
Though hunger, compulsive dread,
Are ghosts forever unlaid
By a moon's impetus
That takes the sea by the throat,
I assert as it gathers up all
Of night to one moment of stress
That is perpetual,
My own self-consciousness.
The waters boom and rave;
Being human what else can I have
Than such good and growing pain,
Between the living and dead,
On this sea-shaken stone?

D. J. ENRIGHT

BORN at Leamington, 1920. Educated Leamington College
and Downing College, Cambridge. Has been an extension
lecturer in England and has lectured abroad in universities
in Berlin, Egypt, Japan and Thailand. At present Professor
of English at Singapore. Works include: *The Laughing
Hyena* (1953); *Bread Rather Than Blossoms* (1956); *Some Men
are Brothers* (1960); *Addictions* (1962); *The Old Adam* (1965).

Humanity in general and the individual man are the
subjects of D. J. Enright's poetry. In viewing as a whole
mankind's problems and future, he never forgets the single
man and woman that make up mankind. The problems of
one man are the problems of mankind. He sees these people
as they appear in their homes—in England, Egypt, Japan,
China. He has faith in them. He looks at them with compassion, sometimes with indignation, and with a sense of
justice which sees what hardship and injustice have done to
them in different places. His irony, a sardonic disengagement, is often turned against himself, more often against the
callousness and hypocrisy that ignore suffering. His language
is spare and colloquial; his rhythms are those of speech with
overtones. His details of observation are sharp and significant. He is one of those

> To whom the miseries of the world
> Are misery, and will not let them rest.

Where Have You Been To? is a fine statement of the predicament of any contemporary poet, with a romantic or nostalgic or mystical streak in him—as have most poets—in a 'levelling, rancorous, rational age'. The subject of the poem might be called the political unreliability of poets or the poetical unreliability of politicians. The poem is a good example of what has been called this poet's 'awkward, honest, serious flippancy'.

Blue Umbrellas

'The thing that makes a blue umbrella with its tail—
How do you call it?' you ask. Poorly and pale
Comes my answer. For all I can call it is peacock.

Now that you go to school, you will learn how we
    call all sorts of things;
How we mar great works by our mean recital.
You will learn, for instance, that Head Monster
    is not the gentleman's accepted title;
The blue-tailed eccentrics will be merely peacocks;
    the dead bird will no longer doze
Off till tomorrow's lark, for the letter has killed him.
The dictionary is opening, the gay umbrellas close.

    Oh our mistaken teachers!—
It was not a proper respect for words that we need,
But a decent regard for things, those older creatures
    and more real.
Later you may even resort to writing verse
To prove the dishonesty of names and their black greed—
To confess your ignorance, to expiate your crime,
    seeking one spell to lift another curse.
Or you may, more commodiously, spy on your children,
    busy discoverers,
Without the dubious benefit of rhyme.

Portrait of the Artist as a Hypocrite

Febrile soul, forever having to recall
That all of what he writes is worse or better
                than the facts.
He, whose tilted nostrils sicken at a smell
That no one else detects,
                speaks for mankind.

One treats of love, and yet he beats his wife.
One hates the human race, yet gives his fees
                to waifs and strays.
Poetry is passion—too many reservations
                break their shooting line,
Who must remember not to give themselves away,
                to editors or women—
Who search a stony contract for their daily bread
                and wine.

The Interpreters

(OR, HOW TO BURY YOURSELF IN A BOOK)

Why have they stripped the grass from the sides
        of the road,
leaving the worms agape, and a senseless load
of brick-ends and broken glass? Tomorrow it will
start to show again. For that is what it means.

One thinks of those critics for whom the outside
    is a dreadful bore:
they scrape for the ambiguous, dig for the profound,
    deep, deep beneath the ground—
what you read on the surface of the agitated page
    is only an idle dusty weed.

The poet mentions suffering and even starvation;
dead cats in the street and women slowly dying on
    the streets;
the lot of a sizeable part of a sizeable nation—
but dear me no!—that will not do for the critic,
    that connoisseur of words
who cannot abide the crude vulgarity of meaning—
his expertise, my dear, merits something richer
than these ancient histories of anguish and horror
    or an empty belly's tasteless keening.

They have sliced the grass away, they are poking
their ingenious lancets in the damp inhuman earth—
around them the blown rice limps to its harvest,
    a child runs to its ambiguous birth,
the peasants look at their rotting cabbages,
a gang of clods are building a block of flats.
But the scholars are chasing a glittering fragment
of Zen or the cracked semblance of an Emblem—
for it is not what a poem merely says that matters,
elsewhere than here it finds its true signification:
    whore, you may be sure,
refers to some mysterious metaphysical temptation;
hunger was his image for a broken dream; bread
an old religious symbol; his typhoons the wind of God.

Good lord, if a poet really meant what he said,
we should all be out of a job—why on earth
would he sing of the merely real?—the papers have
     taken up that chorus—
'the agonies, the strife of human hearts'?—why,
     Hollywood will do that for us.

The peasants have salvaged their cabbages; the block
of flats is nearly as ready as its tenants; somewhere
someone saves a child from a swollen river,
and really means it—
     the critics in their studies, collate as ever
their absences of meanings, unvexing and unvexed—
     but the grass waves high on the road again,
and the roots refer to the text.

The Noodle-Vendor's Flute

In a real city, from a real house,
At midnight by the ticking clocks,
In winter by the crackling roads:
Hearing the noodle-vendor's flute,
Two single fragile falling notes . . .
But what can this small sing-song say,
Under the noise of war?
The flute itself a counterfeit
(Siberian wind can freeze the lips),
Merely a rubber bulb and metal horn
(Hard to ride a cycle, watch for manholes

38

And late drunks, and play a flute together).
Just squeeze between gloved fingers,
And the note of mild hope sounds:
Release, the indrawn sigh of mild despair . . .
A poignant signal, like the cooee
Of some diffident soul locked out,
Less than appropriate to cooling macaroni.
Two wooden boxes slung across the wheel,
A rider in his middle age, trundling
This gross contraption on a dismal road,
Red eyes and nose and breathless rubber horn.
Yet still the pathos of that double tune
Defies its provenance, and can warm
The bitter night.
Sleepless, we turn and sleep.
Or sickness dwindles to some local limb.
Bought love for one long moment gives itself.
Or there a witch assures a frightened child
She bears no personal grudge.
And I, like other listeners,
See my stupid sadness as a common thing.
And being common,
Therefore something rare indeed.
The puffing vendor, surer than a trumpet,
Tells us we are not alone.
Each night that same frail midnight tune
Squeezed from a bogus flute,
Under the noise of war, after war's noise,
It mourns the fallen, every night,
It celebrates survival—
In real cities, real houses, real time.

Where Charity Begins

An old woman squatting, her straight back
   laced against a flimsy lamp-post,
A grey rag bound around her empty eyes—
   she plays a peeling samisen; almost

Unheard, in this city street; she sings
   —what is it? The few who stumble
On her pause a while. A tune before their time,
   tea-house innuendoes in a joyless mumble.

My companion tells me, 'In Peking one night I
   came across a beggar—the only one I saw.
The woman I was with, a foreigner too, gave him
   a little money. I gave a little more.

Some—patriots—saw the act, and disapproved,
   and sent for the police. What could I say?—
That I'd given the man my autograph? Him they
   removed
     to a State Corrective Institution.'

'And you?' 'My chief next morning gave me hell.
   —Respect the custom of the country. When
In Rome . . . Or I'd be begging for my rice, he said.
   I swore I'd not forget myself again.'

Conversing so, we came upon a mother and her nest
   of ragged children scattered in the sun,
A baby fastened to her beaten leather breast—
   sleep, suckle, sweat, they had no time to beg.

A taxi then drew in; another foreigner sprang out.
  He guessed the feet—unwilling to disturb—
Measured the light, and held his camera up and down.
  The indifferent driver waited at the kerb.

Charity. Oh yes, all this we'd seen was charity.
  Make a picture of where your heart once bled,
Move the world's conscience, or provoke an incident—
  all simpler than to fill an empty mouth with bread.

A Polished Performance

Citizens of the polished capital
  Sigh for the towns up country,
And their innocent simplicity.

People in the towns up country
  Applaud the unpolished innocence
Of the distant villages.

Dwellers in the distant villages
  Speak of a simple unspoilt girl,
Living alone, deep in the bush.

Deep in the bush we found her,
  Large and innocent of eye,
Among gentle gibbons and mountain ferns.

Perfect for the part, perfect,
    Except for the dropsy
Which comes from polished rice.

In the capital our film is much admired,
    Its gentle gibbons and mountain ferns,
Unspoilt, unpolished, large and innocent of eye.

Displaced Person looks at a Cage-bird

Every single day, going to where I stay
    (how long?), I pass the canary
In the window. Big bird, all pranked out,
Looming and booming in the window's blank.

Closing a pawky eye, tapping its hairy chest,
    flexing a brawny wing.
Every single day, coming from where I stay
(How long?) I pass this beastly thing.

How I wish it were dead!
    —Florid, complacent, rent-free and over-fed,
Feather-bedded, pensioned, free from wear and tear.
Earth has not anything to show less fair.

I do wish it were dead!
    Then I'd write a better poetry,
On that poor wee bird, its feet in the air,
An innocent victim of something. Just like me.

Dreaming in the Shanghai Restaurant

I would like to be that elderly Chinese gentleman.
He wears a gold watch with a gold bracelet,
But a shirt without sleeves or tie.
He has good luck moles on his face, but is not
        disfigured with fortune.
His wife resembles him, but is still a handsome woman,
She has never bound her feet or her belly.
Some of the party are his children, it seems,
And some his grandchildren;
No generation appears to intimidate another.
He is interested in people, without wanting to
        convert them or pervert them.
He eats with gusto, but not with lust;
And he drinks, but is not drunk.
He is content with his age, which has always suited him.
When he discusses a dish with the pretty waitress,
It is the dish he discusses, not the waitress.
The table-cloth is not so clean as to show indifference,
Not so dirty as to signify lack of manners.
He proposes to pay the bill but knows he will not be
        allowed to.
He walks to the door, like a man who doesn't fret
        about being respected, since he is;
A daughter or grand-daughter opens the door for him,
And he thanks her.
It has been a satisfying evening. Tomorrow
Will be a satisfying morning. In between
        he will sleep satisfactorily.

I guess that for him it is peace in his time.
It would be agreeable to be this Chinese gentleman.

Insects

Chokes in the jungle of my arm,
Diminutive, a dragonfly.
Wealth, not the hollow eyes of want,
This is the vision that must terrify.

Under the smiling lamp
A mass of life lies down to die.
Moths, sample snippets of a finished stamp
—On ivory ground a brush's yellow tip—
Lost wings, the droppings from a master loom.
One spasm ends an epoch's craftsmanship.

If we do not observe, who will?
Will any thing observe or mourn for us?

I wear a beetle, small bronze brooch,
Green-gold the patina of meagre hours,
Against my shirt's coarse twill—
Gaily to meet its death, or ours,
Despite the din of this abstracted mill.

Outside, the night sky hangs above us both,
A giant's foot, free from the smallest cares.
The trees are thickly interlaced:
We elbow through the jungle's choking hairs.

Where Have You Been To?

Into a land of rhythms you had slipped—
Sounds of weathers, songs without words,
Mercurial trees and multithroated birds—
Floated as cloud with other lilting clouds.

Merely the animal noises of your blood,
The blue-grey shallows of tobacco smoke?
Startled, you asked at once when you awoke:
What did it mean, then, what moral for men?

Someone else has stepped in there,
While you were—where?—were elsewhere:
Well-chosen words to sway against or for,
Conventional and nuclear, peace and war.

And you, confused by fading rhythms,
Otherworldly weathers, occult accords and schisms,
Would prove for either side a slippery satellite.

First Death

It is terrible and wonderful: we wake in the strange night
And there is one bed empty and one room full: tears fall,
The children comfort each other, hugging their knees,
        for what will the future be now, poor things?

And next day there is no school, and meals are disorderly,
Things bought from shops, not the old familiar dishes.
New uncles come from far away, soft-voiced strangers
Drinking extraordinary wines. A kind of abstract kindliness
Fills the house, and a smell of flowers. Impossible to be bad—

Other nights pass, under conceded night-lights and a cloud
Of questions: shall we ever go back to school? Ever again
Go to the pictures? Are we too poor for new shoes?
    Must we move
To a council house? Will any of our friends remember us?
Will it always be kind and quiet and sad, like this?

Uncles depart. We go for a week to a country aunt,
Then take a lodger. New shoes are bought—Oh,
    so this is the future!
How long will it last, this time? Never feel safe now.

Mid-Mediterranean September Evening

It is like a smart display of patterns in excellent taste,
And most remarkable is the sense of differing fabrics—
As the sun declines, as clouds affect its shapes and colours,
The sea, the scene, is changed—from tapestry to oilcloth,
Oilcloth to glazed ceramic, to coarse strong carpet work,
And watered silk, stained glass, and back to tapestry.

It is not the commercial blue we are concerned with,
    or the trite designs of foam,

But colours which are textures, textures which are shapes,
And always changing—not with kaleidoscopic jerk like
    soldiers changing guard,
But always a pattern and scheme, and never an empty
    moment while the scene is dressed.

The elongated rainbow eyes, the oily wells, the diamond
    lozenges of purple, brown and blue,
The jellying flanks of blue and black that burst and fuse
    like mercury,
And run along the ship. And now a perfect net of narrow
    squares
That catches the sea tightly, like sleeping leviathan.

And this is the eastern sea.   While on the western plains
The waters are coagulate with huge and vivid colours—
The pattern's lost: with shameless rhetoric the old sun
    makes his exit:
Thunder shakes the gallery: and they are deaf and blind.

The 'Black' Country

'But it is not Black', they will tell you, 'any longer,
    not really Black.'
And of course they have the right ideas, and are right.
Progress is always changing colour: blushes more deeply,
    or now scowls darkly, or turns pale.

True, how can it be called Black?—with its shining cubes
    of metallic branch-groceries,

And the tin gleam of the fish saloon, tiled like a public
    lavatory,
Where the fried fish floats, in Sargasso seas of chips.

It is not Black, in the sense that the desert is Red
With a history of running sores, or that the grass was Green.
Not Black, as Babylon was Scarlet, or the Blood,
As violets are Violet, as Pythagoras' thigh was Golden,
    or corn is—
Not Black as the satin back of this black horse is Black.

So we shall call it the Grey Country, out of deference.
But Grey is slyer than Black: 'Why, I am practically White'.

ROBERT GRAVES

BORN in London, 1895. Educated Charterhouse and St John's College, Oxford. During the First World War served with the Royal Welch Fusiliers in France. Professor of English Literature, Cairo University, 1926. Has lived in Majorca since 1947. Professor of Poetry at Oxford since February 1961. Works include: *Goodbye to All That* (1929) —autobiography; *I, Claudius* (1934)—awarded Hawthornden and James Tait Black Prizes—and *Claudius the God* (1934)—fiction; *Collected Poems* (1938); *Poems 1938–1945* (1946); *The Common Asphodel* (1949)—essays; *Collected Poems* (1959); *More Poems* (1961); *New Poems* (1962); *Love Respect* (1965).

In Robert Graves's poetry there is a combination of a romantic or religious single-mindedness with a tough awareness of and acceptance of the physical, moral and social conditions of life. At the same time, he is classical in his restraint, his logic, his sense of order and his purity of diction. His theme is the relationship of man and woman, of poet and Muse. His poems are often concentrated arguments between the heart, which accepts, and the head, which analyses and rationalizes. In this, he is akin to the Metaphysicals. In his own words, he has two main principles: 'the use of a recognizable metre, and that every word must be given its full meaning'. In his love poems, he accepts the importance of both soul and body, and pays equal homage to affection and physical desire. Each love poem deals with one aspect of love, celebrated and dissected with Metaphysical exactitude and with the wit and honesty of Donne. The love of one man for one woman is treated in such a way that it becomes timeless and eternal in spite of 'Time eating' love and beauty. When he uses a fable as the theme of a poem it is to illuminate a situation of real life.

The Cool Web is close to the heart of the meaning of all Graves's work, typical of him in rhythm, diction, multiple layers of meaning, and the personal flavour of its symbolism. It is a contrast between the innocent and dangerous immediacy of experience, and language as a means of 'making sense' of that immediacy, of controlling it, of keeping it at a safe distance, and therefore making it to a certain extent unreal. Somewhere between inarticulate innocence and the chaos of madness, of 'letting go'—the chaos of 'total recall'—lies the proper terrain of the poet. The metaphors for language, the net and the sea, are peculiarly interesting. Language *is* a 'web', it is a network of relationships that, for men, holds together a multitude of things that, like fish caught in a net, would otherwise swim apart. But *we* are partly the fish; it is language that holds society together, inherited words and concepts that prevent us from achieving a savage independence, that enable the State, when it wants us, to haul us in. (Compare the Ship of State, and St Peter as a fisherman.) But language is not only a network of logical relationships, it is also all the emotive connotations that words carry. It is what holds together not only States and Churches but that vaguer, larger, profounder thing, Human Culture. In that sense it is the sea, what we swim in, where we move and live and have our being. At some level, compared to the heat of the day and the scent of the rose and the drumming of the soldiers, which are 'real' though symbolical in the poem, the sea and the net (or the sea *as* also a net) are 'unreal' or metaphysical; and that suggests the precariousness of the poet's achievement and his situation. The act, more profoundly, of 'spelling away' 'the soldiers and the fright' represents the employment of every possible valid, that is truly felt and self-demonstrable, 'poetic' response in the controlling of experience.

From *Robert Graves* by Martin Seymour-Smith (1956) in the British Council 'Writers and Their Work' Series (by kind permission of Messrs Longmans, Green and Co., Ltd, and the British Council).

1805

At Viscount Nelson's lavish funeral,
   While the mob milled and yelled about St Paul's,
A General chatted with an Admiral:

'One of your Colleagues, Sir, remarked today
   That Nelson's *exit*, though to be lamented,
Falls not inopportunely, in its way.'

'He was a thorn in our flesh,' came the reply—
   'The most bird-witted, unaccountable,
Odd little runt that ever I did spy.

'One arm, one peeper, vain as Pretty Poll,
   A meddler, too, in foreign politics
And gave his heart in pawn to a plain moll.

'He would dare lecture us Sea Lords, and then
   Would treat his ratings as though men of honour
And play at leap-frog with his midshipmen!

'We tried to box him down, but up he popped,
   And when he'd banged Napoleon at the Nile
Became too much the hero to be dropped.

'You've heard that Copenhagen "blind eye" story?
　We'd tied him to Nurse Parker's apron-strings—
By G-d, he snipped them through and snatched the
　glory!'

'Yet,' cried the General, 'six-and-twenty sail
　Captured or sunk by him off Tráfalgár—
That writes a handsome *finis* to the tale.'

'Handsome enough.　The seas are England's now.
　That fellow's foibles need no longer plague us.
He died most creditably, I'll allow.'

'And, Sir, the secret of his victories?'
　'By his unServicelike, familiar ways, Sir,
He made the whole Fleet love him, damn his eyes!'

The Simpleton

To be defrauded often of large sums,
A whole year's income, even,
By friends trusted so long and perfectly
He never thought to ask receipts from them:
Such had been his misfortune.

He did not undervalue money, sighed for
Those banknotes, warm in the breast pocket,
For want of which his plans were baulked;
But could not claim that any man had left him
In complete poverty.

53

Easier to choke back resentment,
Never to sue them, never pit in court
His unsupported oath against theirs;
Easier not to change a forsworn friend
For a sworn enemy.

Easier, too, to scoff at legal safeguards,
Promissories on pale-blue foolscap
Sealed, signed, delivered before witnesses.
What legal safeguard had a full wallet
Carried among a crowd?

But though he preened himself on calmly
Cancelling irrecoverable debts,
It vexed him not to know
Why all his oldest, dearest friends conspired
To pluck him like a fowl.

Here Live Your Life Out!

Window-gazing, at one time or another
In the course of travel, you must have startled at
Some coign of true felicity. 'Stay!' it beckoned,
'Here live your life out!' If you were simple-hearted
The village rose, perhaps, from a broad stream
Lined with alders and gold-flowering flags—
Hills, hayfields, orchards, mills—and, plain to see,
The very house behind its mulberry-tree
Stood, by a miracle, untenanted!

Alas, you could not alight, found yourself jolted
Viciously on; public conveyances
Are not amenable to casual halts
Except in sternly drawn emergencies—
Bandits, floods, landslides, earthquakes or the like—
Nor could you muster resolution enough
To shout: 'This is emergency, let me out!',
Rushing to grasp their brakes; so the whole scene
Withdrew for ever. Once at the terminus
(As your internal mentor will have told you),
It would have been pure folly to engage
A private car, drive back, sue for possession.
Too far, too late:
Already bolder tenants were at the gate.

Warning to Children

Children, if you dare to think
Of the greatness, rareness, muchness,
Fewness of this precious only
Endless world in which you say
You live, you think of things like this:
Blocks of slate enclosing dappled
Red and green, enclosing tawny
Yellow nets, enclosing white
And black acres of dominoes,
Where a neat brown paper parcel
Tempts you to untie the string.
In the parcel a small island,

On the island a large tree,
On the tree a husky fruit.
Strip the husk and pare the rind off:
In the kernel you will see
Blocks of slate enclosed by dappled
Red and green, enclosed by tawny
Yellow nets, enclosed by white
And black acres of dominoes,
Where the same brown paper parcel—
Children, leave the string untied!
For who dares undo the parcel
Finds himself at once inside it,
On the island, in the fruit,
Blocks of slate about his head,
Finds himself enclosed by dappled
Green and red, enclosed by yellow
Tawny nets, enclosed by black
And white acres of dominoes,
With the same brown paper parcel
Still unopened on his knees.
And, if he then should dare to think
Of the fewness, muchness, rareness,
Greatness of this endless only
Precious world in which he says
He lives—he then unties the string.

Lollocks

By sloth on sorrow fathered,
These dusty-featured Lollocks

Have their nativity in all disordered
Backs of cupboard drawers.

They play hide and seek
Among collars and novels
And empty medicine bottles,
And letters from abroad
That never will be answered.

Every sultry night
They plague little children,
Gurgling from the cistern,
Humming from the air,
Skewing up the bed-clothes,
Twitching the blind.

When the imbecile agèd
Are over-long in dying
And the nurse drowses,
Lollocks come skipping
Up the tattered stairs
And are nasty together
In the bed's shadow.

The signs of their presence
Are boils on the neck,
Dreams of vexation suddenly recalled
In the middle of the morning,
Langour after food.

Men cannot see them,
Men cannot hear them,

Do not believe in them—
But suffer the more,
Both in neck and belly.

Women can see them—
O those naughty wives
Who sit by the fireside
Munching bread and honey,
Watching them in mischief
From corners of their eyes,
Slily allowing them to lick
Honey-sticky fingers.

Sovereign against Lollocks
Are hard broom and soft broom,
To well comb the hair,
To well brush the shoe,
And to pay every debt
As it falls due.

The Cool Web

Children are dumb to say how hot the day is,
How hot the scent is of the summer rose,
How dreadful the black wastes of evening sky,
How dreadful the tall soldiers drumming by.

But we have speech, to chill the angry day,
And speech, to dull the rose's cruel scent.

We spell away the overhanging night,
We spell away the soldiers and the fright.

There's a cool web of language winds us in,
Retreat from too much joy or too much fear:
We grow sea-green at last and coldly die
In brininess and volubility.

But if we let our tongues lose self-possession,
Throwing off language and its watery clasp
Before our death, instead of when death comes,
Facing the wide glare of the children's day,
Facing the rose, the dark sky and the drums,
We shall go mad no doubt and die that way.

Dialogue on the Headland

SHE: You'll not forget these rocks and what I told you?
HE: How could I? Never: whatever happens.
SHE: What do you think might happen?
  Might you fall out of love?—did you mean that?
HE: Never, never! 'Whatever' was a sop
  For jealous listeners in the shadows.
SHE: You haven't answered me. I asked:
  'What do you think might happen?'
HE: Whatever happens: though the skies should fall
  Raining their larks and vultures in our laps—
SHE: 'Though the seas turn to slime'—say that—
  'Though water-snakes be hatched with six heads.'

HE :   Though the seas turn to slime, or tower
        In an arching wave above us, three miles high—
SHE :   'Though she should break with you',—dare you say
            that?—
        'Though she deny her words on oath.'
HE :   I had that in my mind to say, or nearly;
        It hurt so much I choked it back.
SHE :   How many other days can't you forget?
        How many other loves and landscapes?
HE :   You are jealous?
SHE :   Damnably.
HE :   The past is past.
SHE :   And this?
HE :   Whatever happens, this goes on.
SHE :   Without a future? Sweetheart, tell me now:
        What do you want of me? I must know that.
HE :   Nothing that isn't freely mine already.
SHE :   Say what is freely yours and you shall have it.
HE :   Nothing that, loving you, I could dare take.
SHE :   O, for an answer with no 'nothing' in it!
HE :   Then give me everything that's left.
SHE :   Left after what?
HE :   After whatever happens:
        Skies have already fallen, seas are slime,
        Watersnakes poke and peer six-headedly—
SHE :   And I lie snugly in the Devil's arms.
HE :   I said: 'Whatever happens.' Are you crying?
SHE :   You'll not forget me—ever, ever, ever?

Mid-Winter Waking

Stirring suddenly from long hibernation,
I knew myself once more a poet
Guarded by timeless principalities
Against the worm of death, this hillside haunting;
And presently dared open both my eyes.

O gracious, lofty, shone against from under,
Back-of-the-mind-far clouds like towers;
And you, sudden warm airs that blow
Before the expected season of new blossom,
While sheep still gnaw at roots and lambless go—

Be witness that on waking, this mid-winter,
I found her hand in mine laid closely
Who shall watch out the Spring with me.
We stared in silence all around us
But found no winter anywhere to see.

The Terraced Valley

In a deep thought of you and concentration
I came by hazard to a new region:
The unnecessary sun was not there,
The necessary earth lay without care—
For more than sunshine warmed the skin
Of the round world that was turned outside-in.

Calm sea beyond the terraced valley
Without horizon easily was spread,
As it were overhead,
Washing the mountain-spurs behind me:
The unnecessary sky was not there,
Therefore no heights, no deeps, no birds of the air.

Neat outside-inside, neat below-above,
Hermaphrodizing love.
Neat this-way-that-way and without mistake:
On the right hand could slide the left glove.
Neat over-under: the young snake
Through an unyielding shell his path could break.
Singing of kettles, like a singing brook,
Made out-of-doors a fireside nook.

But you, my love, where had you then your
        station?
Seeing that on this counter-earth together
We go not distant from each other;
I knew you near me in that strange region,
So searched for you, in hope to see you stand
On some near olive-terrace in the heat,
The left-hand glove drawn on your right hand,
The empty snake's egg perfect at your feet—

But found you nowhere in the wide land,
And cried disconsolately, until you spoke
Immediate at my elbow, and your voice broke
This trick of time, changing the world about
To once more inside-in and outside-out.

The Foreboding

Looking by chance in at the open window
  I saw my own self seated in his chair
With gaze abstracted, furrowed forehead,
  Unkempt hair.

I thought that I had suddenly come to die,
  That to a cold corpse this was my farewell,
Until the pen moved slowly upon paper
  And tears fell.

He had written a name, yours, in printed letters:
  One word on which bemusedly to pore—
No protest, no desire, your naked name,
  Nothing more.

Would it be tomorrow, would it be next year?
  But the vision was not false, this much I knew;
And I turned angrily from the open window
  Aghast at you.

Why never a warning, either by speech or look,
  That the love you cruelly gave me could not last?
Already it was too late: the bait swallowed,
  The hook fast.

THOM GUNN

Born at Gravesend, 1929. Educated University College School, London, and Trinity College, Cambridge. Lecturer for the University of California at Berkeley. Works: *Fighting Terms* (1954); *The Sense of Movement* (1957); *My Sad Captains* (1961); *Positives* (1966).

Starting in his first book with love poems, in which love was a struggle and a problem—as the whole of life was to become to him in his later poems—Thom Gunn has widened his themes in later books. His questioning of life and of himself leads him to the conclusion that uncertainty is the only certain thing. Tough and realistic, but at the same time logical and intellectual, he dissects the conditions of life today in startling metaphors and images. The result is a poetry as contemporary and realistic as Donne's was, and moving in its very topicality and energy and economy of phrase. His most original and ambitious poem, *On the Move*, takes as its subject the 'tough' black-leather-jacketed boys on motor-cycles, who symbolize action and violence without motive.

On the Move

'Man, you gotta Go'

The blue jay scuffling in the bushes follows
Some hidden purpose, and the gust of birds
That spurts across the field, the wheeling swallows,
Have nested in the trees and undergrowth.
Seeking their instinct, or their poise, or both,
One moves with an uncertain violence
Under the dust thrown by a baffled sense
Or the dull thunder of approximate words.

On motor-cycles, up the road, they come:
Small, black, as flies hanging in heat, the Boys,
Until the distance throws them forth, their hum
Bulges to thunder held by calf and thigh.
In goggles, donned impersonality,
In gleaming jackets trophied with the dust,
They strap in doubt—by hiding it, robust—
And almost hear a meaning in their noise.

Exact conclusion of their hardiness
Has no shape yet, but from known whereabouts
They ride, direction where the tires press.
They scare a flight of birds across the field:

66

Much that is natural, to the will must yield.
Men manufacture both machine and soul,
And use what they imperfectly control
To dare a future from the taken routes.

It is a part solution, after all.
One is not necessarily discord
On earth; or damned because, half animal,
One lacks direct instinct, because one wakes
Afloat on movement that divides and breaks.
One joins the movement in a valueless world,
Choosing it, till, both hurler and the hurled,
One moves as well, always toward, toward.

A minute holds them, who have come to go:
The self-defined, astride the created will
They burst away; the towns they travel through
Are home for neither bird nor holiness,
For birds and saints complete their purposes.
At worst, one is in motion; and at best,
Reaching no absolute, in which to rest,
One is always nearer by not keeping still.

Human Condition

Now it is fog, I walk
Contained within my coat;
No castle more cut off
By reason of its moat:

Only the sentry's cough,
The mercenaries' talk.

The street lamps, visible,
Drop no light on the ground,
But press beams painfully
In a yard of fog around.
I am condemned to be
An individual.

In the established border
There balances a mere
Pinpoint of consciousness.
I stay, or start from, here:
No fog makes more or less
The neighbouring disorder.

Particular, I must
Find out the limitation
Of mind and universe,
To pick thought and sensation
And turn to my own use
Disordered hate or lust.

I seek, to break, my span.
I am my one touchstone.
This is a test more hard
Than any ever known.
And thus I keep my guard
On that which makes me man.

Much is unknowable.
No problem shall be faced
Until the problem is;
I, born to fog, to waste,
Walk through hypothesis,
An individual.

Tamer and Hawk

I though I was so tough,
But gentled at your hands
Cannot be quick enough
To fly for you and show
That when I go I go
At your commands.

Even in flight above
I am no longer free:
You seeled me with your love,
I am blind to other birds—
The habit of your words
Has hooded me.

As formerly, I wheel
I hover and I twist,
But only want the feel,
In my possessive thought,
Of catcher and of caught
Upon your wrist.

You but half-civilize,
Taming me in this way.
Through having only eyes
For you I fear to lose,
I lose to keep, and choose
Tamer as prey.

My Sad Captains

One by one they appear in
the darkness: a few friends, and
a few with historical
names. How late they start to shine!
but before they fade they stand
perfectly embodied, all

the past lapping them like a
cloak of chaos. They were men
who, I thought, lived only to
renew the wasteful force they
spent with each hot convulsion.
They remind me, distant now.

True, they are not at rest yet,
but now that they are indeed
apart, winnowed from failures,
they withdraw to an orbit
and turn with disinterested
hard energy, like the stars.

The Middle of the Night

Open, box, for the child
Who lifts out, one by one,
Impudent and self-willed
Dolls from the living heap
—Their antics never done
Which took him from his sleep.

Lion and citizen,
Soldier in pose of fight,
A wicker stork, small men,
Small gods and animals . . . .
The box is emptied out:
The floor is bright with dolls.

Year after year the same,
A town of perfect size.
Who calls it a mere game?
Round him, alive and shrunk
Each finished burgher lies,
Whose cargoes have been sunk.

He learns their histories—
Jerk, posture, giggle, prance,
And grows to recognize
In each doll, passive, faded,
Some man who is at once
Transfigured and degraded.

At length he writes it down,
Recording what befalls
Until the dark is gone.
Children who know by heart
The vices of their dolls
Will stay awake at night.

Considering the Snail

The snail pushes through a green
night, for the grass is heavy
with water and meets over
the bright path he makes, where rain
has darkened the earth's dark. He
moves in a wood of desire,

pale antlers barely stirring
as he hunts. I cannot tell
what power is at work, drenched there
with purpose, knowing nothing.
What is a snail's fury? All
I think is that if later

I parted the blades above
the tunnel and saw the thin
trail of broken white across
litter, I would never have
imagined the slow passion
to that deliberate progress.

First Meeting with a Possible Mother-in-law

She thought, without the benefit of knowing,
You, who had been hers, were not any more.
We had locked our love in to leave nothing showing
From the room her handiwork had crammed before;
But—much revealing in its figured sewing—
A piece of stuff hung out, caught in the door.
I caused the same suspicion I watched growing:
Who could not tell what whole the part stood for?

There was small likeness between her and me:
Two strangers left upon a bare top landing,
I for a prudent while, she totally.

But, eyes turned from the bright material hint,
Each shared too long a second's understanding,
Learning the other's terms of banishment.

Flying above California

Spread beneath me it lies—lean upland
sinewed and tawny in the sun, and

valley cool with mustard, or sweet with
loquat. I repeat under my breath

names of places I have not been to:
Crescent City, San Bernardino

—Mediterranean and Northern names.
Such richness can make you drunk. Sometimes

on fogless days by the Pacific,
there is a cold hard light without break

that reveals merely what is—no more
and no less. That limiting candour,

that accuracy of the beaches,
is part of the ultimate richness.

The Silver Age

Do not enquire from the centurion nodding
At the corner, with his head gentle over
The swelling breastplate, where true Rome is found.
Even of Livy there are volumes lost.
All he can do is guide you through the moonlight.

When he moves, mark how his eager striding,
To which we know the darkness is a river
Sullen with mud, is easy as on ground.
We know it is a river never crossed
By any but some few who hate the moonlight.

And when he speaks, mark how his ancient wording
Is hard with indignation of a lover.
'I do not think our new Emperor likes the sound
Of turning squadrons or the last post.
Consorts with Christians, I think he lives in moonlight.'

Hurrying to show you his companions guarding,
He grips your arm like a cold strap of leather,
Then halts, earthpale, as he stares round and round.
What made this one fragment of a sunken coast
Remain, far out, to be beaten by the moonlight?

TED HUGHES

BORN at Mytholmroyd in the West Riding of Yorkshire, 1930. Educated Mexborough Grammar School and Pembroke College, Cambridge. Works: *The Hawk in the Rain* (1957); *Lupercal* (1960); *Meet My Folks* (1961)—verse for children.

The natural world is the ostensible subject of much of Ted Hughes's poetry. He describes, with insight and imagination, the world as a wild creature might see it—an otter, a hawk, a jaguar, an owl, a pike, a fox—but he finds in these creatures, in their beauty, greed, instinctive and untameable violence, and lust for survival, images of the passionate energies of man. They illustrate and symbolize and illuminate human life and experience and qualities in human beings that cannot be domesticated. His limited and personal themes are broadened to throw light on many things of importance in the contemporary world of terror and uncertainty. His comparatively narrow range of images, violent and compelling, sensuous and highly visual, is made relevant to contemporary life. His sympathy and compassion for the world of the untamed is twofold: for itself and for it as a symbol of man. His language is lucid, bold, vigorous, even violent, uncompromising and unsentimental. His tone is harsh and tough. But humanity and tenderness underline all his poems. In *Woman Unconscious*, he unsentimentally sets against the contemporary threat of world destruction the fact that we all die anyway, and alone.

In *Hawk Roosting*, the life of the bird is seized in essence; the bird is the centre, the epitome, of creation. The bird is untameable; the violence of bird life is stated in the brute physical facts of blood and action. The bird is used as a way to explore the poet's sense of life, to define the range and intensity of his instincts by dramatizing them. The blind instinctive thrust (in itself an image of terror) of the animal world is paradoxically an image of the terror of our contemporary world, where evolution and mankind have produced means to destroy itself. The language is strong and precise, exact and muscular. The energy is held in check, the violence is under control.

The Thought-Fox

I imagine this midnight moment's forest:
Something else is alive
Beside the clock's loneliness
And this blank page where my fingers move.

Through the window I see no star:
Something more near
Though deeper within darkness
Is entering the loneliness:

Cold, delicately as the dark snow,
A fox's nose touches twig, leaf;
Two eyes serve a movement, that now
And again now, and now, and now

Sets neat prints into the snow
Between trees, and warily a lame
Shadow lags by stump and in hollow
Of a body that is bold to come

Across clearings, an eye,
A widening deepening greenness,
Brilliantly, concentratedly,
Coming about its own business

Till, with a sudden sharp hot stink of fox
It enters the dark hole of the head.
The window is starless still; the clock ticks,
The page is printed.

The Jaguar

The apes yawn and adore their fleas in the sun.
The parrots shriek as if they were on fire, or strut
Like cheap tarts to attract the stroller with the nut.
Fatigued with indolence, tiger and lion

Lie still as the sun. The boa-constrictor's coil
Is a fossil. Cage after cage seems empty, or
Stinks of sleepers from the breathing straw.
It might be painted on a nursery wall.

But who runs like the rest past these arrives
At a cage where the crowd stands, stares, mesmerized,
As a child at a dream, at a jaguar hurrying enraged
Through prison darkness after the drills of his eyes

On a short fierce fuse. Not in boredom—
The eye satisfied to be blind in fire,
By the bang of blood in the brain deaf the ear—
He spins from the bars, but there's no cage to him

More than to the visionary his cell:
His stride is wilderness of freedom:
The world rolls under the long thrust of his heel.
Over the cage floor the horizons come.

Hawk Roosting

I sit in the top of the wood, my eyes closed.
Inaction, no falsifying dream
Between my hooked head and hooked feet:
Or in sleep rehearse perfect kills and eat.

The convenience of the high trees!
The air's buoyancy and the sun's ray
Are of advantage to me;
And the earth's face upward for my inspection.

My feet are locked upon the rough bark.
It took the whole of Creation
To produce my foot, my each feather:
Now I hold Creation in my foot

Or fly up, and revolve it all slowly—
I kill where I please because it is all mine.
There is no sophistry in my body:
My manners are tearing off heads—

The allotment of death.
For the one path of my flight is direct
Through the bones of the living.
No arguments assert my right:

The sun is behind me.
Nothing has changed since I began.
My eye has permitted no change.
I am going to keep things like this.

To Paint a Water Lily

A green level of lily leaves
Roofs the pond's chamber and paves

The flies' furious arena: study
These, the two minds of this lady.

First observe the air's dragonfly
That eats meat, that bullets by

Or stands in space to take aim;
Others as dangerous comb the hum

Under the trees. There are battle-shouts
And death-cries everywhere hereabouts

But inaudible, so the eyes praise
To see the colours of these flies

Rainbow their arcs, spark, or settle
Cooling like beads of molten metal

Through the spectrum. Think what worse
Is the pond-bed's matter of course;

Prehistoric bedragonned times
Crawl that darkness with Latin names,

Have evolved no improvements there,
Jaws for heads, the set stare,

Ignorant of age as of hour—
Now paint the long-necked lily-flower

Which, deep in both worlds, can be still
As a painting, trembling hardly at all

Though the dragonfly alight,
Whatever horror nudge her root.

October Dawn

October is marigold, and yet
A glass half full of wine left out

To the dark heaven all night, by dawn
Has dreamed a premonition

Of ice across its eye as if
The ice-age had begun its heave.

The lawn overtrodden and strewn
From the night before, and the whistling green

Shrubbery are doomed. Ice
Has got its spearhead into place.

First a skin, delicately here
Restraining a ripple from the air;

Soon plate and rivet on pond and brook;
Then tons of chain and massive lock

To hold rivers. Then, sound by sight
Will Mammoth and Sabre-tooth celebrate

Reunion while a fist of cold
Squeezes the fire at the core of the world,

Squeezes the fire at the core of the heart,
And now it is about to start.

Wind

This house has been far out at sea all night,
The woods crashing through darkness, the booming hills,
Winds stampeding the fields under the window
Floundering black astride and blinding wet

Till day rose; then under an orange sky
The hills had new places, and wind wielded
Blade-light, luminous and emerald,
Flexing like the lens of a mad eye.

At noon I scaled along the house-side as far as
The coal-house door. I dared once to look up—
Through the brunt wind that dented the balls of my eyes
The tent of the hills drummed and strained its guyrope,

The fields quivering, the skyline a grimace,
At any second to bang and vanish with a flap:
The wind flung a magpie away and a black-
Back gull bent like an iron bar slowly. The house

Rang like some fine green goblet in the note
That any second would shatter it. Now deep
In chairs, in front of the great fire, we grip
Our hearts and cannot entertain book, thought,

Or each other. We watch the fire blazing,
And feel the roots of the house move, but sit on,
Seeing the window tremble to come in,
Hearing the stones cry out under the horizons.

Pennines in April

If this county were a sea (that is solid rock
Deeper than any sea) these hills heaving
Out of the east, mass behind mass, at this height
Hoisting heather and stones to the sky
Must burst upwards and topple into Lancashire.

Perhaps, as the earth turns, such ground-stresses
Do come rolling westward through the locked land.
Now, measuring the miles of silence
Your eye takes the strain: through

Landscapes gliding blue as water
Those barrellings of strength are heaving slowly
    and heave
To your feet and surf upwards
In a still, fiery air, hauling the imagination,
Carrying the larks upward.

A Woman Unconscious

Russia and America circle each other;
Threats nudge an act that were without doubt
A melting of the mould in the mother,
Stones melting about the root.

The quick of the earth burned out:
The toil of all our ages a loss
With leaf and insect. Yet flitting thought
(Not to be thought ridiculous)

Shies from the world-cancelling black
Of its playing shadow: it has learned
That there's no trusting (trusting to luck)
Dates when the world's due to be burned;

That the future's no calamitous change
But a malingering of now,
Histories, towns, faces that no
Malice or accident much derange.

And though bomb be matched against bomb,
Though all mankind wince out and nothing endure—
Earth gone in an instant flare—
Did a lesser death come

Onto the white hospital bed
Where one, numb beyond her last of sense,
Closed her eyes on the world's evidence
And into pillows sunk her head.

A Dream of Horses

We were born grooms, in stable-straw we sleep still,
All our wealth horse-dung and the combings of horses,
And all we can talk about is what horses ail.

Out of the night that gulfed beyond the palace-gate
There shook hooves and hooves and hooves of horses:
Our horses battered their stalls; their eyes jerked white.

And we ran out, mice in our pockets and straw in our hair,
Into darkness that was avalanching to horses
And a quake of hooves. Our lantern's little orange flare

Made a round mask of our each sleep-dazed face,
Bodiless, or else bodied by horses
That whinnied and bit and cannoned the world from its
    place.

The tall palace was so white, the moon was so round,
Everything else this plunging of horses
To the rim of our eyes that strove for the shapes of the
    sound.

We crouched at our lantern, our bodies drank the din,
And we longed for a death trampled by such horses
As every grain of the earth had hooves and mane.

We must have fallen like drunkards into a dream
Of listening, lulled by the thunder of the horses.
We awoke stiff; broad day had come.

Out through the gate the unprinted desert stretched
To stone and scorpion; our stable-horses
Lay in their straw, in a hag-sweat, listless and wretched.

Now let us, tied, be quartered by these poor horses,
If but doomsday's flames be great horses,
The forever itself a circling of the hooves of horses.

My Grandpa

The truth of the matter, the truth of the matter—
As one who supplies us with hats is a Hatter,
As one who is known for his growls is a Growler—
My grandpa traps owls, yes, my grandpa's an Owler.

Though owls, alas, are quite out of fashion,
Grandpa keeps busy about his profession

And hoards every owl that falls to his traps:
'Someday,' says he, 'they'll be needed, perhaps.'

'Owls are such sages,' he says, 'I surmise
Listening to owls could make the world wise.'
Nightlong his house is shaken with hoots,
And he wakes to owls in his socks and his boots.

Owls, owls, nothing but owls,
The most fantastical of fowls:
White owls from the Arctic, black owls from the Tropic.
Some are far-sighted, others myopic.

There are owls on his picture frames, owls on his chairs,
Owls in dozens ranked on his stairs.
Eyes, eyes, rows of their eyes.
Some are big as collie dogs, some are thumb-size.

Deep into Africa, high into Tibet
He travels with his rubber mouse and wiry owl-net:
The rarest of owls, and the very most suspicious
Will pounce on the mouse and be tangled in the meshes.

'Whatever you could wish to know, an owl will surely
    know it,'
My grandpa says proudly. 'And how does he show it?
Sleeping and thinking and sleeping and thinking—
Letting a horrible hoot out and winking!'

PATRICK KAVANAGH

୧୬୫୪୬

1905–67. Born in County Monaghan, Eire. Educated Common National School. Left school at thirteen. 'Squandered next ten years.' Under the influence of 'A. E.' began to write verse. Has tramped all over Ireland. Works: *Ploughman and Other Poems* (1936); *The Green Fool* (1938)—an autobiography; *The Great Hunger* (1942); *A Soul for Sale* (1947); *Tarry Flynn* (1948)—fiction; *Come Dance with Kitty Stobling* (1960); *Collected Poems* (1963).

Patrick Kavanagh's poetry is steeped in the atmosphere of the farm in County Monaghan where he grew up and worked. Apparently naïve but with much subtlety of intellect and imagination, his poems explore the world round him, and the greater world, from this firmly rooted basis. Many of his poems celebrate the virtues and blessings of what is—especially in the natural world. He is honest and does not pose; he is original and unpretentious. He views himself with the same mockery that he views others, the so-called important men of this world. He digs deeply, like R. S. Thomas, if not widely, in his poems, and they are consequently alive and moving. The casual ease of his colloquial style is an integral part of his poetry. In *Canal Bank Walk*, by a slight twist of heavy sermonizing, he is able to suggest the unfathomable significance of living creatures.

Is

The important thing is not
To imagine one ought
Have something to say,
A raison d'être, a plot for the play.
The only true teaching
Subsists in watching
Things moving or just colour
Without comment from the scholar.
To look on is enough
In the business of love.
Casually remark
On a deer running in a park;
Mention water again
Always virginal,
Always original,
It washes out Original Sin.
Name for the future
The everydays of nature
And without being analytic
Create a great epic.
Girls in red blouses,
Steps up to houses,
Sunlight round gables,
Gossip's young fables,
The life of a street.

O wealthy me! O happy state!
With an inexhaustible theme
I'll die in harness,
I'll die in harness with my scheme.

Intimate Parnassus

Men are what they are, and what they do
Is their own business. If they praise
The gods or jeer at them, the gods can not
Be moved, involved or hurt. Serenely
The citizens of Parnassus look on
As Homer tells us, and never laugh
When any mortal has joined the party.
What happens in the small towns—
Hate, love, envy—is not
The concern of the gods. The poet poor
Or pushed around, or to be hanged, retains
His full reality; and his authority
Is bogus if the sonorous beat is broken
By disturbances in human hearts—his own
Is detached, experimental, subject matter
For ironic analysis, even for pity
As for some stranger's private problem.
It is not cold on the mountain, human women
Fall like ripe fruit while mere men
Are climbing out on dangerous branches
Of banking, insurance and shops; going
To the theatre; becoming

Acquainted with actors; unhappily
Pretending to a knowledge of art.
Poet, you have reason to be sympathetic—
Count them the beautiful unbroken
And then forget them
As things aside from the main purpose
Which is to be
Passive, observing with a steady eye.

If ever you go to Dublin town

If ever you go to Dublin town
In a hundred years or so
Inquire for me in Baggot Street
And what I was like to know.
O he was a queer one
Fol dol the di do,
He was a queer one
I tell you.

My great-grandmother knew him well,
He asked her to come and call
On him in his flat and she giggled at the thought
Of a young girl's lovely fall.
O he was dangerous
Fol dol the di do,
He was dangerous
I tell you.

On Pembroke Road look out for my ghost
Dishevelled with shoes untied,
Playing through the railings with little children
Whose children have long since died.
O he was a nice man
Fol dol the di do,
He was a nice man
I tell you.

Go into a pub and listen well
If my voice still echoes there,
Ask the men what their grandsires thought
And tell them to answer fair.
O he was eccentric
Fol dol the di do,
He was eccentric
I tell you.

He had the knack of making men feel
As small as they really were
Which meant as great as God had made them
But as males they disliked his air.
O he was a proud one
Fol dol the di do,
He was a proud one
I tell you.

If ever you go to Dublin town
In a hundred years or so
Sniff for my personality,
Is it vanity's vapour now?

O he was a vain one
Fol dol the di do,
He was a vain one
I tell you.

I saw his name with a hundred others
In a book in the library
It said he had never fully achieved
His potentiality.
O he was slothful
Fol dol the di do,
He was slothful
I tell you.

He knew that posterity has no use
For anything but the soul,
The lines that speak the passionate heart,
The spirit that lives alone.
O he was a lone one
Fol dol the di do,
Yet he lived happily
I tell you.

Living in the Country

OPENING

It was the warm Summer, that landmark
In a child's mind, an infinite day
Sunlight and burnt grass
Green grasshoppers on the railway slopes

The humming of wild bees
The whole summer during the school holidays
Till the blackberries appeared.
Yes, a tremendous time that summer stands
Beyond the grey finities of normal weather.

THE MAIN BODY

It's not nearly as bad as you'd imagine
Living among small farmers in the north of Ireland
They are for the most part the ordinary frightened
Blind brightened, referred to sometimes socially
As the underprivileged.
They cannot perceive Irony or even Satire
They start up with insane faces if
You break the newspaper moral code.
'Language' they screech 'you so and so'
And you withdraw into a precarious silence
Organizing in your mind quickly, for the situation is tense,
The theological tenets of the press.

There's little you can do about some
Who roar horribly as you enter a bar
Incantations of ugliness, words of half a syllable
Locked in malicious muteness full of glare.
And your dignity thinks of giving up the beer.

But I trained in the slum pubs of Dublin
Among the most offensive class of all—
The artisans—am equal to this problem;
I let it ride and there is nothing over.
I understand through all these years

That my difference in their company is an intrusion
That tears at the sentimental clichés
They can see my heart squirm when their star rendites
The topmost twenty in the lowered lights.
No sir, I did not come unprepared.

Oddly enough I begin to think of Saint Francis
Moving in this milieu (of his own time of course)
How did he work the oracle?
Was he an old fraud, a non-poet
Who is loved for his non-ness
Like any performer?

I protest here and now and forever
On behalf of all my peoples who believe in Verse
That my intention is not satire but humaneness
An eagerness to understand more about sad man
Frightened man, the workers of the world
Without being savaged in the process.
Broadness is my aim, a broad road where the many
Can see life easier—generally.

Here I come to a sticky patch
A personal matter that perhaps
Might be left as an unrevealed hinterland
For our own misfortunes are mostly unimportant.
But that wouldn't do.
So with as little embarrassment as possible I tell
How I was done out of a girl,
Not as before by a professional priest but by
The frightened artisan's morality.

It was this way.
She, a shopgirl of nineteen or less
Became infatuated by the old soldier,
The wide travelled the sin-wise.
Desdemona–Othello idea.
O holy spirit of infatuation
God's gift to his poetic nation!

One day her boss caught her glance.
'You're looking in his eyes' he said.
From then all the powers of the lower orders—
Perhaps all orders—were used to deprive me of my prize
Agamemnon's Briseis.
It soured me a bit as I had
Everything planned, no need to mention what,
Except that it was August evening under whitethorn
And early blackberries.

In many ways it is a good thing to be cast into exile
Among strangers
Who have no inkling
Of The Other Man concealed
Monstrously musing in a field.
For me they say a Rosary
With many a glossary.

Primrose

Upon a bank I sat, a child made seer
Of one small primrose flowering in my mind.
Better than wealth it is, said I, to find
One small page of Truth's manuscript made clear.
I looked at Christ transfigured without fear—
The light was very beautiful and kind,
And where the Holy Ghost in flame had signed
I read it through the lenses of a tear.
And then my sight grew dim, I could not see
The primrose that had lighted me to Heaven,
And there was but the shadow of a tree
Ghostly among the stars. The years that pass
Like tired soldiers nevermore have given
Moments to see wonders in the grass.

Canal Bank Walk

Leafy-with-love banks and the green waters of the canal
Pouring redemption for me, that I do
The will of God, wallow in the habitual, the banal,
Grow with nature again as before I grew.
The bright stick trapped, the breeze adding a third
Party to the couple kissing on an old seat,
And a bird gathering materials for the nest for the Word
Eloquently new and abandoned to its delirious beat.

O unworn world enrapture me, encapture me in a web
Of fabulous grass and eternal voices by a beech,
Feed the gaping need of my senses, give me ad lib
To pray unselfconsciously with overflowing speech
For this soul needs to be honoured with a new dress woven
From green and blue things and arguments that cannot be
    proven.

October

O leafy yellowness you create for me
A world that was and now is poised above time,
I do not need to puzzle out Eternity
As I walk this arboreal street on the edge of a town.
The breeze too, even the temperature
And pattern of movement is precisely the same
As broke my heart for youth passing. Now I am sure
Of something. Something will be mine wherever I am.
I want to throw myself on the public street without caring
For anything but the prayering that the earth offers.
It is October over all my life and the light is staring
As it caught me once in a plantation by the fox coverts.
A man is ploughing ground for winter wheat
And my nineteen years weigh heavily on my feet.

Peace

And sometimes I am sorry when the grass
Is growing over the stones in quiet hollows
And the cocksfoot leans across the rutted cart-pass
That I am not the voice of country fellows
Who now are standing by some headland talking
Of turnips and potatoes or young corn
Or turf banks stripped for victory.
Here Peace is still hawking
His coloured combs and scarves and beads of horn.

Upon a headland by a whinny hedge
A hare sits looking down a leaf-lapped furrow
There's an old plough upside-down on a weedy ridge
And someone is shouldering home a saddle-harrow.
Out of that childhood country what fools climb
To fight with tyrants Love and Life and Time?

Shancoduff

My black hills have never seen the sun rising,
Eternally they look north towards Armagh.
Lot's wife would not be salt if she had been
Incurious as my black hills that are happy
When dawn whitens Glassdrummond chapel.

My hills hoard the bright shillings of March
While the sun searches in every pocket.
They are my Alps and I have climbed the Matterhorn
With a sheaf of hay for three perishing calves
In the field under the Big Forth of Rocksavage.

The sleety winds fondle the rushy beards of Shancoduff
While the cattle-drovers sheltering in the Featherna Bush
Look up and say: 'Who owns them hungry hills
That the water-hen and snipe must have forsaken?
A poet? Then by heavens he must be poor.'
I hear and is my heart not badly shaken?

Literary Adventures

I am here in a garage in Monaghan,
It is June and the weather is warm,
Just a little bit cloudy. There's the sun again
Lifting to importance my sixteen acre farm.
There are three swallows nests in the rafter above me
And the first clutches are already flying.
Spread this news, tell all if you love me,
You who knew that when sick I was never dying.
(Nae gane, nae gane, nae frae us torn
But taking a rest like John Jordan)
                    Other exclusive
News stories that cannot be ignored:
I climbed Woods' Hill and the elusive
Underworld of the grasses could be heard,

John Lennon shouted across the valley.
Then I saw a New June Moon, quite as stunning
As when young we blessed the sight as something
     holy . . .
Sensational adventure that is only beginning.

For I am taking this evening walk through places
High up among the Six Great Wonders
The power privileges, the unborn amazes
The unplundered
Where man with no meaning blooms
Large in the eyes of his females
He doesn't project, nor even assumes
The loss of one necessary believer.
It's as simple as that, it's a matter
Of walking with the little gods, the ignored
Who are so seldom asked to write the letter
Containing the word.
O only free gift! no need for Art any more
When Authority whispers like tyranny at the end of a
     bar.

In Memory of My Mother

I do not think of you lying in the wet clay
Of a Monaghan graveyard; I see
You walking down a lane among the poplars
On your way to the station, or happily

Going to second Mass on a summer Sunday—
You meet me and you say:
'Don't forget to see about the cattle—'
Among your earthiest words the angels stray.

And I think of you walking along a headland
Of green oats in June,
So full of repose, so rich with life—
And I see us meeting at the end of a town

On a fair day by accident, after
The bargains are all made and we can walk
Together through the shops and stalls and markets
Free in the oriental streets of thought.

O you are not lying in the wet clay,
For it is a harvest evening now and we
Are piling up the ricks against the moonlight
And you smile up at us—eternally.

LOUIS MacNEICE

1907-63. Born in Belfast. The son of the Bishop of Down, Connor, and Dromore. Educated Marlborough and Merton College, Oxford. Lecturer in Classics Birmingham University, 1931. Lecturer in Greek, Bedford College, London, 1936. A member of the staff of the B.B.C., engaged in writing and producing radio plays and features from 1941 to 1949. Director of the British Institute at Athens, 1950. Works include: *Poems* (1935); *Letters from Iceland* (1937)—with W. H. Auden; *The Earth Compels* (1938); *Autumn Journal* (1939); *Plant and Phantom* (1941); *Springboard* (1944); *The Dark Tower* (1947)—radio plays; *Holes in the Sky* (1948); *Collected Poems* 1925-1948 (1949); *Ten Burnt Offerings* (1952); *Autumn Sequel* (1954); *Visitations* (1957); *Solstices* (1961); *The Burning Pestle* (1963); *The Strings are False* (1965)—autobiography; *Collected Poems* (1966).

From his classical training Louis MacNeice has gained lucidity, reasonableness, a sense of order, and skill in prosody. To these qualities he has added the Irishman's talkativeness and interest in everything, and the journalist's vivid sense of people and landscapes, his immediacy and topicality, and his fear of being 'taken in'. This disillusionment gives satirical toughness and energy to his verse, which draws sustenance from love and nature and travel and the 'number of things that fill the world'. Although of an earlier generation, he accepts the life of today; as he says about his latest volume, 'These are poems of acceptance, even of joy.' His flair is for taking a simple observation, fact, incident, or situation, and for developing it to a point where it acquires a new symbolic meaning—e.g., in a poem where the mindless movement of a windscreen wiper starts him reflecting upon continuity and survival. His poetry expresses his sense of continuing, at all costs, to exist. To this sense contribute the many facets of life that are the subjects of his poetry—childhood memories, landscapes, character sketches of people and places, personal reflections, fables of yesterday and today, celebrations of love and happiness. Whether his subject is a personal impression or a human problem, the mood is evoked with ingenuity and clarity, intelligence and wit. He says of his later verse that the poems are more concentrated and better organized, 'relying more on syntax and bony feature than on bloom or frill or the floating image'.

To Posterity

When books have all seized up like the books in graveyards
And reading and even speaking have been replaced
By other, less difficult, media, we wonder if you
Will find in flowers and fruit the same colour and taste
They held for us for whom they were framed in words,
And will your grass be green, your sky be blue,
Or will your birds be always wingless birds?

Solstice

How did midsummer come so soon,
The lean trees racing into lush?
He had turned his back one moment, then turned
And took it full in the face—the gush
Of green, the stare of blue, the sieve
Of sun and shadow, the wish to live.

And what was nowhere now was here
And here was all and all was good;
Between the lines the words were strange
Yet not to be misunderstood.
The glad flowers talked with tongues of flame
And who was he was not the same.

Nor was there question who was she
For whom his years were blessed to wait,
Whose opening eyes to him were now,
As his to hers, an open gate,
One entrance to one constant song.
How can midsummer stay so long?

Meeting Point

Time was away and somewhere else
There were two glasses and two chairs
And two people with the one pulse
(Somebody stopped the moving stairs):
Time was away and somewhere else.

And they were neither up nor down
The stream's music did not stop
Flowing through heather, limpid brown,
Although they sat in a coffee shop
And they were neither up nor down.

The bell was silent in the air
Holding its inverted poise—
Between the clang and clang a flower,
A brazen calyx of no noise:
The bell was silent in the air.

The camels crossed the miles of sand
That stretched around the cups and plates;
The desert was their own, they planned
To portion out the stars and dates:
The camels crossed the miles of sand.

Time was away and somewhere else.
The waiter did not come, the clock
Forgot them and the radio waltz
Came out like water from a rock:
Time was away and somewhere else.

Her fingers flicked away the ash
That bloomed again in tropic trees:
Not caring if the markets crash
When they had forests such as these,
Her fingers flicked away the ash.

God or whatever means the Good
Be praised that time can stop like this,
That what the heart has understood
Can verify in the body's peace
God or whatever means the Good.

Time was away and she was here
And life no longer what it was,
The bell was silent in the air
And all the room a glow because
Time was away and she was here.

Reflections

The mirror above my fireplace reflects the reflected
Room in my window; I look in the mirror at night
And see two rooms, the first where left is right
And the second, beyond the reflected window, corrected
But there I am standing back to my back. The standard
Lamp comes thrice in my mirror, twice in my window,
The fire in the mirror lies two rooms away through the
    window,
The fire in the window lies one room away down the
    terrace,
My actual room stands sandwiched between confections
Of night and lights and glass and in both directions
I can see beyond and through the reflections the street lamps
At home outdoors where my indoors rooms lie stranded,
Where a taxi perhaps will drive in through the bookcase
Whose books are not for reading and past the fire
Which gives no warmth and pull up by my desk
At which I cannot write since I am not lefthanded.

Nature Notes

DANDELIONS

Incorrigible, brash,
They brightened the cinder path of my childhood,
Unsubtle, the opposite of primroses,
But, unlike primroses, capable

112

Of growing anywhere, railway track, pierhead,
Like our extrovert friends who never
Make us fall in love, yet fill
The primroseless roseless gaps.

CATS

Incorrigible, uncommitted,
They leavened the long flat hours of my childhood,
Subtle, the opposite of dogs,
And, unlike dogs, capable
Of flirting, falling, and yawning anywhere,
Like women who want no contract
But going their own way
Make the way of their lovers lighter.

CORNCRAKES

Incorrigible, unmusical,
They bridged the surrounding hedge of my child-
    hood,
Unsubtle, the opposite of blackbirds,
But, unlike blackbirds, capable
Anywhere they are of endorsing summer
Like loud men around the corner
Whom we never see but whose raucous
Voices can give us confidence.

THE SEA

Incorrigible, ruthless,
It rattled the shingly beach of my childhood,

Subtle, the opposite of earth,
And, unlike earth, capable
Any time at all of proclaiming eternity
Like something or someone to whom
We have to surrender, finding
Through that surrender life.

Sunday Morning

Down the road someone is practising scales,
The notes like little fishes vanish with a wink of tails,
Man's heart expands to tinker with his car
For this is Sunday morning, Fate's great bazaar;
Regard these means as ends, concentrate on this Now,
And you may grow to music or drive beyond Hindhead
    anyhow,
Take corners on two wheels until you go so fast
That you can clutch a fringe or two of the windy past,
That you can abstract this day and make it to the week of
    time
A small eternity, a sonnet self-contained in rhyme.

But listen, up the road, something gulps, the church spire
Opens its eight bells out, skulls' mouths which will not tire
To tell how there is no music or movement which secures
Escape from the weekday time. Which deadens and
    endures.

Birmingham

Smoke from the train-gulf hid by hoardings blunders
  upward, the brakes of cars
Pipe as the policeman pivoting round raises his flat hand,
  bars
With his figure of a monolith Pharaoh the queue of fidgety
  machines
(Chromium dogs on the bonnet, faces behind the triplex
  screens).
Behind him the streets run away between the proud glass
  of shops,
Cubical scent-bottles artificial legs arctic foxes and electric
  mops,
But beyond this centre the slumward vista thins like a
  diagram:
There, unvisited, are Vulcan's forges who doesn't care a
  tinker's damn.

Splayed outwards through the suburbs houses, houses for
  rest
Seducingly rigged by the builder, half-timbered houses with
  lips pressed
So tightly and eyes staring at the traffic through bleary haws
And only a six-inch grip of the racing earth in their concrete
  claws;
In these houses men as in a dream pursue the Platonic Forms
With wireless and cairn terriers and gadgets approximating
  to the fickle norms
And endeavour to find God and score one over the neigh-
  bour

By climbing tentatively upward on jerry-built beauty and
    sweated labour.

The lunch hour: the shops empty, shopgirls' faces relax
Diaphanous as green glass, empty as old almanacs,
As incoherent with ticketed gewgaws tiered behind their
    heads
As the Burne-Jones windows in St Philip's broken by
    crawling leads;
Insipid colour, patches of emotion, Saturday thrills
(This theatre is sprayed with 'June')—the gutter take our
    old playbills,
Next weekend it is likely in the heart's funfair we shall pull
Strong enough on the handle to get back our money; or at
    any rate it is possible.

On shining lines the trams like vast sarcophagi move
Into the sky, plum after sunset, merging to duck's egg,
    barred with mauve
Zeppelin clouds, and Pentecost-like the cars' headlights bud
Out from sideroads and the traffic signals, crême-de-menthe
    or bull's blood,
Tell one to stop, the engine gently breathing, or to go on
To where like black pipes of organs in the frayed and fading
    zone
Of the West the factory chimneys on sullen sentry will all
    night wait
To call, in the harsh morning, sleep-stupid faces through the
    daily gate.

Wessex Guidebook

Hayfoot; strawfoot; the illiterate seasons
Still clump their way through Somerset and Dorset
While George the Third still rides his horse of chalk
From Weymouth and the new salt water cure
Towards Windsor and incurable madness. Inland
The ghosts of monks have grown too fat to walk
Through bone-dry ruins plugged with fossil sea-shells.

Thou shalt! Thou shalt not! In the yellow abbey
Inscribed beneath the crossing the Ten Commandments
Are tinted red by a Fifteenth Century fire;
On one round hill the yews still furnish bows
For Agincourt while, equally persistent,
Beneath another, in green-grassed repose,
Arthur still waits the call to rescue Britain.

Flake-tool; core-tool; in the small museum
Rare butterflies, green coins of Caracalla,
Keep easy company with the fading hand
Of one who chronicled a fading world;
Outside, the long roads, that the Roman ruler
Ruled himself out with, point across the land
To lasting barrows and long vanished barracks.

And thatchpoll numskull rows of limestone houses,
Dead from the navel down in plate glass windows,
Despise their homebrewed past, ignore the clock
On the village church in deference to Big Ben

Who booms round china dog and oaken settle
Announcing it is time and time again
To plough up tumuli, to damn the hindmost.

But hindmost, topmost, those illiterate seasons
Still smoke their pipes in swallow-hole and hide-out
As scornful of the tractor and the jet
As of the Roman road, or axe of flint,
Forgotten by the mass of human beings
Whom they, the Seasons, need not even forget
Since, though they fostered man, they never loved him.

Day of Returning

But even so, he said, daily I hanker, daily
Ache to get back to my home, to see my day of returning
After those years of violent action—and these of inaction.
Always and even so. But I have no ship, no comrades,
Only my wits with nothing to grind on. Nectar, ambrosia,
Promise me nothing; the goddess no longer pleases me.
Who would be loved by a goddess for long? Hours which
     are golden
But unreal hours, flowers which forget to fall,
And wine too smooth, no wrinkles to match my own—
Who would be loved by a goddess who cannot appreciate
The joy of solving a problem, who never wept
For friends that she used to laugh with? I stare at the sea
Till that hard horizon rounds one great round eye
Hard as that of the Cyclops; this time I have no

Means of putting it out—and now I am really No Man
For my ears ring with a too sweet voice which never
Falters or ages. They call me crafty Odysseus;
I have used my craft on gods and nymphs and demigods
But it is time, high time, I turned it again
To the earth that bred it, a new threshing floor
Or setting up boundary stones, for even the best
Neighbours encroach—and I like to have someone to argue
    with
About my rights of grazing or wood-cutting; aye, it is time
I heard the bleat of my goats and smelt the dung of my
    cattle;
Here there is neither dung nor rights nor argument,
Only the scent of flowers and a too sweet voice which is
    ever
Youthful and fails to move me. Here could never be home,
No more than the sea around it. And even the sea
Is a different sea round Ithaca.

VERNON SCANNELL

BORN in Lincolnshire, 1922. Educated at an elementary
school in Aylesbury, and Leeds University, where he was
Captain of Boxing. Joined the Gordon Highlanders in 1940,
and served in the Middle East and Normandy. A free-lance
and a part-time teacher. Works include: *A Mortal Pitch*
(1957); *The Masks of Love* (1960)—given the Heineman
Award for Literature; *A Sense of Danger* (1962); *The Fight,
The Face of the Enemy*, and *The Dividing Night* (1962)—
fiction; *Walking Wounded* (1963); edited (with Ted Hughes
and Patricia Beer) *New Poems 1962* (the P.E.N. Anthology).

Vernon Scannell, like another novelist-poet, Thomas
Hardy, often puts into verse an incident of everyday life,
and in his choice of incident he prefers, again like Hardy,
to combine the violent and the macabre with the ordinary.
He tells the story in simple metre and in everyday words,
economical of phrase. But out of this everyday incident or
trite situation—an anniversary, a silver wedding, a biographical entry, an unanswered telephone call—comes a
profound truth or a flash of insight into some problem of
mankind. Frequently the poem echoes a feeling of in-
security: the poet's fear of the present and the future (and
the past), his doubt of the demarcation between reality and
illusion, his uncertainty of his own identity, his horror at

'man's inhumanity to man', his dread of the atavistic primitive in man. But against these stands his belief in the kindness, heroism and innocence of man. Like the Metaphysicals, he says that he 'wants a poem to contain wit, passion, hard thinking and delicate feeling'; and, again like the Metaphysicals, his attitude is often one of irony, of sardonic disengagement.

Hearthquake shows the isolation of the individual in fear. Of *Biographical Note*, the poet has been careful to say that it is not autobiographical but fictional. The subject of *Lesson in Grammar* defines the moral basis of human life in terms of a lesson: life must make sense and must be based on the right relationship with others. The deliberately casual style heightens the earnestness of purpose. The mildly humorous manner of a schoolmaster obviates any taint of preaching.

Makers and Creatures

It is a curious experience
And one you're bound to know, though probably
In other realms than that of literature,
Though I speak of poems now, assuming
That you are interested, otherwise,
Of course, you wouldn't be reading this.
It is strange to come across a poem
In an old magazine, perhaps, and fail
At first to see that it's your own.
Sometimes you think, grateful and surprised,
'That's really not too bad', or gloomily:
'Many have done as well and far, far better'.
Or, in despair, 'My God that's terrible.
What was I thinking of to publish it'.
And then you start to wonder how the great
Poets felt, seeing, surprised, their poems
As strangers, beautiful. And how do all the
Makers feel to see their creatures live:
The carpenter, the architect, the man who
Crochets intricate embroideries
Of steel across the sky. And how does God
Feel, looking at his poems, his creatures?
The swelling inhalation of plump hills,
Plumage of poplars on the pale horizon,
Fishleap flashing in pools cool as silver,

Great horses haunched with glossy muscles
And birds who spray their song like apple juice
And the soft shock of snow. He must feel good
Surprised again by these. But what happens
When He takes a look at Man? Does He say,
'That's really not too bad', Or does He, as I fear,
Wince ruefully and mutter to Himself:
'What was I thinking of publishing that one'?

Biographical Note

Born in 1920. Educated
At various schools and an ancient university
At which he studied History and edited
A magazine of verse. Served in the infantry.
Has worked as journalist and schoolmaster;
Now lives in the country with his wife and little daughter.

And there we have him, pinned like petal or moth
At the end of a feverish anthology
Which has not long to live, nor will be missed.
But I, who know him well, can tell you this:
His life has never been, and is not now,
As cosy as these dead-pan facts allow.

About his birth I cannot speak except
To mention that he often cursed its hour.
The various schools were branches of one trunk
Bleak, bare, stripped of leaf and flower:

His one year at the university was fine;
He walked in vigorous showers and tried to gather
Sprays of sparkling sounds, but the year was '39.
He put on clothes that stank of their dark colour
And studied new techniques in formal murder
But lacked the needed skills and shook all over
When meaty corporals steamed with hot invective.
In martial talents he was found defective.

As journalist his lance was free but no
Barons hired it, which was just as well,
For nature had not cast him for a mercenary;
Teaching was a journey back to hell.
The rural home's a sty; his wife a soft
White moaner and his daughter, tinted pink,
Is vociferous and cruel. And he—well, he
Does not complain and manages to laugh
And seems, in fact, to love his family.
But what amazes most, he works away
At wretched stints to earn their bread and broth,
Tending his small gift, fragile as petal or moth.

A City Remembered

Unlovely city, to which few tourists come
With squinting cameras and alien hats;
Left under a cloud by those who love the sun
And can afford to marry—a cloud of bits
Of soot more myriad than gnats, a cloud

Of smoke and rain, an insubstantial threat
Whose colour is the pigment of long wrath,
I think of you, surprised to find my blood
Warmed by a wry desire, a kind of love.
I see the trams, like galleons at night,
Go rocking with their golden cargo down
The iron hills; then hearing that bold din
My other senses frolic at a fête
Of phantom guests—the smells of fish and chips,
Laborious smoke, stale beer and autumn gusts,
The whispering shadows and the winking hips,
The crack of frosty whips, brief summer's dust.
And in that city through a forked November
Love, like a catherine-wheel, delighted me
And when it sputtered out, hung charred and sombre,
The city flavoured my delicious misery.
And so I guess that any landscape's beauty
Is fathered by associative joys
Held in a shared, historic memory,
For beauty is the shape of our desires.
My northern city, then, by many called
Ugly or worse, much like an aged nurse
Tender yet stern who taught one how to walk,
Is dear to me, and it will always have
A desolate enchantment that I'll love.

Autobiographical Note

Beeston, the place, near Nottingham:
We lived there for three years or so.

Each Saturday at two-o'clock
We queued up for the matinée,
All the kids for streets around
With snotty noses, giant caps,
Cut down coats and heavy boots,
The natural enemies of cops
And schoolteachers. Profane and hoarse
We scrambled, yelled and fought until
The Picture Palace opened up
And we, like Hamelin children, forced
Our bony way into the hall.
That much is easy to recall;
Also the reek of chewing-gum,
Gob-stoppers and liquorice,
But of the flickering myths themselves
Not much remains. The hero was
A milky wide-brimmed hat, a shape
Astride the arched white stallion;
The villain's horse and hat were black.
Disbelief did not exist
And laundered virtue always won
With quicker gun and harder fist,
And all of us applauded it.
Yet I remember moments when
In solitude I'd find myself
Brooding on the sooty man,
The bristling villain, who could move
Imagination in a way
The well-shaved hero never could,
And even warm the nervous heart
With something oddly close to love.

They did not expect this

They did not expect this. Being neither wise nor brave
And wearing only the beauty of youth's season
They took the first turning quite unquestioningly
And walked quickly without looking back even once.

It was of course the wrong turning. First they were nagged
By a small wind that tugged at their clothing like a dog;
Then the rain began and there was no shelter anywhere,
Only the streets and the rows of houses stern as soldiers.

Though the blood chilled, the endearing word burnt
        the tongue.
There were no parks or gardens or public houses:
Midnight settled and the rain paused leaving the city
Enormous and still like a great sleeping seal.

At last they found accommodation in a cold
Furnished room where they quickly learnt to believe in
        ghosts;
They had their hope stuffed and put on the mantelpiece
But found, after a while, that they did not notice it.

While she spends many hours looking in the bottoms of
        teacups
He reads much about association football
And waits for the marvellous envelope to fall:
Their eyes are strangers and they rarely speak.
                    They did not expect this.

Silver Wedding

The party is over and I sit among
The flotsam that its passing leaves,
The dirty glasses and fag-ends:
Outside, a black wind grieves.

Two decades and a half of marriage;
It does not really seem as long,
And yet I find I have scant knowledge
Of youth's ebullient song.

David, my son, my loved rival,
And Julia, my tapering daughter,
Now grant me one achievement only:
I turn their wine to water.

And Helen, partner of all these years,
Helen, my spouse, my sack of sighs,
Reproaches me for every hurt
With injured, bovine eyes.

There must have been passion once, I grant,
But neither she nor I could bear
To have its ghost come prowling from
Its dark and frowsy lair.

And we, to keep our nuptials warm,
Still wage sporadic, fireside war;
Numb with insult each yet strives
To scratch the other raw.

Twenty-five years we've now survived;
I'm not sure either why or how
As I sit with a wreath of quarrels set
On my tired and balding brow.

Ageing Schoolmaster

And now another autumn morning finds me
    With chalk dust on my sleeve and in my breath,
Preoccupied with vague, habitual speculation
    On the huge inevitability of death.

Not wholly wretched, yet knowing absolutely
    That I shall never reacquaint myself with joy,
I sniff the smell of ink and chalk and my mortality
    And think of when I rolled, a gormless boy,

And rollicked round the playground of my hours,
    And wonder when precisely tolled the bell
Which summoned me from summer liberties
    And brought me to this chill autumnal cell

From which I gaze upon the april faces
    That gleam before me, like apples ranged on shelves,
And yet I feel no pinch or prick of envy
    Nor would I have them know their sentenced selves.

With careful effort I can separate the faces,
    The dull, the clever, the various shapes and sizes,
But in the autumn shades I find I only
    Brood upon death, who carries off all the prizes.

Schoolroom on a Wet Afternoon

The unrelated paragraphs of morning
Are forgotten now; the severed heads of kings
Rot by the misty Thames; the roses of York
And Lancaster are pressed between the leaves
Of history; negroes sleep in Africa.
The complexities of simple interest lurk
In inkwells and the brittle sticks of chalk:
Afternoon is come and English Grammar.

Rain falls as though the sky has been bereaved,
Stutters its inarticulate grief on glass
Of every lachrymose pane. The children read
Their books or make pretence of concentration,
Each bowed head seems bent in supplication
Or resignation to the fate that waits
In the unmapped forests of the future.
Is it their doomed innocence noon weeps for?

In each diminutive breast a human heart
Pumps out the necessary blood: desires,
Pains and ecstasies surf-ride each singing wave
Which breaks in darkness on the mental shores.
Each child is disciplined; absorbed and still
At his small desk. Yet lift the lid and see,
Amidst frayed books and pencils, other shapes:
Vicious rope, glaring blade, the gun cocked to kill.

Lesson in Grammar

Perhaps I can make it plain by analogy.
Imagine a machine, not yet assembled,
Each part being quite necessary
To the functioning whole: if the job is fumbled
And a vital piece mislaid
The machine is quite valueless,
The workers will not be paid.

It is just the same when constructing a sentence
But here we must be very careful
And lay stress on the extreme importance
Of defining our terms: nothing is as simple
As it seems at first regard.
'Sentence' might well mean to you
The amorous rope or twelve years' hard.

No, by 'sentence' we mean, quite simply, words
Put together like the parts of a machine.
Now remember we must have a verb: verbs
Are words of action like Murder, Love, or Sin.
But these might be nouns, depending
On how you use them—
Already the plot is thickening.

Except when the mood is imperative; that is to say
A command is given like Pray, Repent, or Forgive
(Dear me, these lessons get gloomier every day)

Except, as I was saying, when the mood is gloomy—
    I mean imperative
We need nouns, or else of course
Pronouns; words like Maid,
Man, Wedding or Divorce.

A sentence must make sense. Sometimes I believe
Our lives are ungrammatical. I guess that some of
    you
Have misplaced the direct object: the longer I live
The less certain I feel of anything I do.
But now I begin
To digress. Write down these simple sentences:—
I am sentenced: I love: I murder: I sin.

Hearthquake

A week has passed without a word being said:
No headlines, though that's natural, I suppose,
Since there were no injured, let alone dead,
Yet I expected a paragraph or so.
But no, not even comment passed in bars,
No gossip over fences while shirts flap
And sheets boast on the line like sails on spars,
And yet it happened; I can swear to that.
I remember it as if it were last night,
My sitting smug and cosy as a cat
Until the carpet suddenly took fright

And bucked beneath my feet. Walls winced. The clock
Upon the mantelpiece began to dance;
The photograph of me aged twenty-one fell flat;
Glass cracked. The air went cold with shock.
I did not sleep at all well through that night
Nor have I since. I cannot understand
Why no one—not my nearest neighbour even—
Refers to what occurred on that strange evening
Unless, in some way difficult to see,
He is afraid to mention it. Like me.

The Ambush

Noise paled, gradual or quick, I cannot say,
And I became aware of silence everywhere;
I sucked it in when I breathed in the air.

Silence lay inside my lungs and heart
And in my brain. And with the silence came
A stillness such as paintings would disclaim.

This rural scene was not a work of art:
The fallen tree lay in real bluebells while
It played at being an actual crocodile.

The sky was real, the brambles like barbed wire
Would scratch and snag the clothing or the skin;
This Surrey wood seemed one for wandering in.

But I did not go in though I had meant to.
I waited for a whisper, cry or screech.
The whole green parliament had stifled speech.

Irresolute I waited there until
The hostile death of noise sent me away;
I swore that I'd return on a more propitious day.

But safe in the dangerous noises of the city
I knew I'd never know what thing hid there,
What voiceless incarnation of despair

Or vigilant guerilla lying still,
With breath indrawn among the ferns and dirt,
Waiting to attack or be dealt his mortal hurt.

A Sense of Danger

The city welcomed us. Its favoured sons,
Holders of office, prosperous and plump
With meat and honours, said, 'Put down your guns,
There's nothing here to fear. The industrial slump,
The Plague, the hunting-packs, the underfed,
All are gone, all caged or safely dead.

'Rest easy here. Put down your loads and stay,
And we will purify you with the kiss
Of sweet hygienic needles and display
Incredible varieties of bliss;

We'll strip your inhibitions off like trousers.
Relax. Don't brood. You'll be as safe as houses'.

But we declined, took up our guns and bags;
Turning blind backs on offers of delight
Left for the gaunt terrain and squinting crags;
With luck we'd find a water-hole that night.
'As safe as houses' they had called the town;
But we had seen great houses tumbled down.

The Terrible Abstractions

The naked hunter's fist, bunched round his spear,
Was tight and wet inside with sweat of fear;
He heard behind him what the hunted hear.

The silence in the undergrowth crept near;
Its mischief tickled in his nervous ear
And he became the prey, the quivering deer.

The naked hunter feared the threat he knew:
Being hunted, caught, then slaughtered like a ewe
By beasts who padded on four legs or two.

The naked hunter in the bus or queue
Under his decent wool is frightened too
But not of what his hairy forebear knew.

The terrible abstractions prowl about
The compound of his fear and chronic doubt;
He keeps fires burning boldly all night through,
But cannot keep the murderous shadows out.

Incendiary

That one small boy with a face like pallid cheese
And burnt-out little eyes could make a blaze
As brazen, fierce and huge, as red and gold
And zany yellow as the one that spoiled
Three thousand guineas worth of property
And crops at Godwin's Farm on Saturday
Is frightening—as fact and metaphor:
An ordinary match intended for
The lighting of a pipe or kitchen fire
Misused may set a whole menagerie
Of flame-fanged tigers roaring hungrily.
And frightening, too, that one small boy should set
The sky on fire and choke the stars to heat
Such skinny limbs and such a little heart
Which would have been content with one warm kiss
Had there been anyone to offer this.

The Men Who Wear My Clothes

Sleepless I lay last night and watched the slow
    Procession of the men who wear my clothes:
First, the grey man with bloodshot eyes and sly
    Gestures miming what he loves and loathes.

Next came the cheery knocker-back of pints,
  The beery joker, never far from tears
Whose loud and public vanity acquaints
  The careful watcher with his private fears.

And then I saw the neat-mouthed gentle man
  Defer politely, listen to the lies,
Smile at the tedious talk and gaze upon
  The little mirrors in the speaker's eyes.

The men who wear my clothes walked past my bed
  And all of them looked tired and rather old;
I felt a chip of ice melt in my blood.
  Naked I lay last night and very cold.

HAL SUMMERS

Born in Bradford, 1911. Educated Fettes and Trinity College, Oxford. Civil Servant. Works: *Smoke after Flame* (1944); *Hinterland* (1947); *Visions of Time* (1952).

With something of the analytical method of Donne, Hal Summers explores the intricacies of human relationships, especially those of lovers. He brings a probing and alert mind to the situations of day-by-day living, and reveals depths visible only to a poet in ordinary human experiences. At the heart of the storm he finds a calm and a quietude. He sees into the mind of the child and of the old, and he views both with detachment and with compassion. His verse form is simple, yet adapted to its subject, and his economy of phrase matches its exactitude.

Seeds of Song

Thrown on neglected earth
The seeds of song lie hid
Like things of little worth
Of which the world is rid.

Their tender nurse is then
The wild and winter snows
And the blind beating rain;
Where they lie no one knows.

When other creatures grow
And the bare boughs are leaved
They sleep, and are as though
They had not been conceived.

And time will out of these
Raise up so great a crop,
The all-kindled chestnut trees
Will cower beneath their top.

At my first look

At my first look, long ago now, a child,
I loved the natural world, sometimes was wild
With longing to possess, impossibly,
Its heart of sweetness; then by sympathy
Not only would my joy leap at sunshine,
The sun too, seemed, would leap for joy of mine.
Mild rain relieved my griefs, I would engraft
My mirth to grow on pear-trees when I laughed.
Once on a bright morning the sun caught glints
From distant garden frames, starched cotton prints
Flapped on a clothes-line, crocuses were thick,
A cock crew, larks sang: was delight a trick
Of mood, or from the outward world beginning?
I ask now—then the question had no meaning.

Then later, smarting with some adult pain,
Nothing was bitterer than the high disdain
Of sumptuous seasons: flowers were gaudiest then
Like tactless visitors of dying men.
Salt in my raw hurt rankled daylight's flavour;
Sweet, on a tooth's nerve, sagged the hyacinth's savour.
If noise of running brooks could turn unkind
What comfort could be certain? I divined
That nether skies are of all skies most blue
And for the damned the sun is burning too.
Tantalus drinks his draught, he does not thirst,
The river is cool about him: o the worst
Of the rebellious angels for their sin
Were not cast out of heaven, they were kept in.

But now, having seen something and heard of more,
Informed of perfect goodness in the core,
And spider's lust, and intrigue of the weevil,
And physical cruelty, the pit of evil,
I turn back, and again on nature look
And find clouds, earth, rain, mountains, tree and brook
Different, good in themselves, but not concerned
With our play, no theme's counterpoint, not turned
As cyclorama or revolving stage;
We are their background rather: them no age
Compromises, their hearts can never break
Nor fail at filthy violence; they make
Final truth which no further inference carries;
Glorious like poems, not like commentaries.

The Seed

I am the small million,
I am the locked fountain.

Late, late in summer's dotage
When they lie gaunt and blasted,
The hollyhock tower and the cottage
Of clover, and age has wasted
The sun—then, then at last
I jump, I glide, a waif
Victoriously lost,
Tempestuously safe.

I go as weak as seawater,
I lie as quiet as radium.

In the dust-high caravan, in
The cabin of a bird's claw
Or sheepback I travel, I have been
In the whale's prophesying maw.
I have occupied both town
And parish, an air-borne spirit, a
Soldier in thistledown,
A meek inheritor.

I am dry but I shall slake you,
I am hard but I shall satisfy you.

The apple contains me and I
Contain the apple, I balance
A field on a stalk and tie
A century's voices in silence,
And all the hopes of the happy
And all the sighs of the sorry
Rest in my power to copy
And copying vary.

I am the first omega,
I am the last alpha.

And remember, I lie beneath
All soils of time, fears' frost,
Remember, I stir in my death,
Most missed I am least lost,

Remember, in the gaunt garden,
In the kingdom of a broken tree,
You will find after Armageddon,
After the deluge, me.

The Scene

The scene is a corner of a lane in summer,
One side rank nettles and behind them
A mound of cut grass decomposing.
The hedges both sides are of thorn
Whitened with dust; a sharp right turn
Takes off the road uphill. There is a ditch
Where water-beetles walk with burnished backs
On the other side, and in lush grass and chervil
A palpitating frog looks out at me.
Behind the lower hedge, ploughland well grown,
And the ground still falls to far-divided fields
Where a square church tower rises.
Behind the other hedge
A straggled field with two holly-trees in it
And a well worn diagonal path
Leads up towards a cottage. It is three o'clock,
I am alone, the sun shines,
No bird sings. Silver vapours
Rise slowly from the earth
And in this windless corner
The tasseled nettles cluster close and dark
And the heap of dead grass sends out an acrid smell.

That is the scene, you say. And so, what happened?
O nothing—nothing happened nor shall ever happen.
The background is the picture, the stage is the play.
This scene, hot and empty of the afternoon,
Shall lie sequestered in my book's corner;
No foot of man shall ever cross it,
And certainly no wheeled vehicle shall cross it,
Nor any aircraft cast a shadow on it.
The page shall be for ever warm and empty with it,
It shall be idle and silent and smelling of nettles and
    dead grass;
And it shall live.

The Yorkshire Moors

The pearls of a day hung in the topmost height
When my crested hope whistled over drybuilt walls
And I over the good peat and the moss-green bog
Wandered my never-lost way between the calls

Of curlew and playing plover; that was of all
The emptiest world that ever I striding saw,
With a blank road running in the tireless hills
And a day's money to spend, day without flaw.

The heather was young yet and the bilberry leaves
Grew green in the burnt places, bracken was curled
In that flowerless paradise—the stones were the flowers
And the sepal and petal of brilliant water whirled

Under the crag; and over by Ilkley way
I counted, line upon line, rack over rack
The nameless moors I would never walk, and a certain
Concourse of light and cloud which would never come back.

On the Cliff

Cloud-riders leap for Normandy,
The opulent sun in his grandstand
Looks on, the dark and shaggy sea
Worries the white bone of the land.

Who made me an arbiter? May I
Not follow as wind and season lead?
There is no verdict in the sky
Nor in the growing of the seed.

The mind of nature changes ever,
Ever renews: o let me yield
My rigid thought, flow as a river
Or rivery shadows on the weald;

Live like the blossom on these branches
Flaming and falling as times pass
Or like the obedient moon that blanches
The unrebellious fields of grass;

With children's welcome see the day
Closing the volume of the dark
And listen in the innocent way
To the high quavers of the lark;

Passive let me, when blind night fingers
Its braille of stars, that light receive
While in my ear unchallenged lingers
The owl's lugubrious semibreve.

Clouds at the water-jump fly fraught
With hazardous light: come good or ill,
Ring off now, rest, protesting thought.
And let the judging mind be still.

A Valentine

At one point of the journey, a memorable one,
The train ran out of the tunnel under the down
And look, it was a new country, we had outrun
All vestige at last of the pursuing town.

The train ran quietly under a sky of jade;
There could not be a metropolis under that sky;
Each side was a hanging field of such deep shade
It was the mind greened it and not the eye.

At the moment a thing seems memorable, and yet
Though the memory be retentive and true the heart,
We begin almost immediately to forget;
The sand-castle is washed away, part by part.

Then there is another moment: I open the door,
Enter the lighted house, out of the weather,
And look, a new country—this I journeyed for:
I come to you, speak to you, we are together.

This moment also and so all moments fade,
Like a piano's chord, loud, evanescent.
Waves of brightness rill into cold shade.
We can be safe neither in past nor present.

Love calls continually for life's whole power;
Either it must be renewed or it must die.
Each hour we are new souls: o love, each hour
Meet me the first time, say me last good-bye.

Thoughts in Absence

Set free the dove from the housetop.
She flies: in the street below,
In the steel-framed eyes of the windows
Not one of them seems to know.

She is lost in the fume and smoke
And the murderous cars run hot;
A city's snake-hair of wires
Reaches out to catch at her throat.

I send this dove to my love
But I cannot tell her the way:
I tell her, go into danger
Since here you must not stay.

I send this dove from the ark
Where she must never touch down:
Either she finds her tree to sit
Or she finds her wave to drown.

Set free the dove from the housetop.
Send out the dove from the ark.
I free her, I send her, I shall not know
If she finds my love, her mark.

O Dowland, old John Dowland

O Dowland, old John Dowland, make a tune for this,
Two lovers married, like to turtle-doves,
Whose mutual eyes no curtain knew nor shade their kiss
And fruitful with a child their holiday loves.

Set that to harmony and then beside it set
Heaven steeled with armament and nations bent
On conquest and resistance, the unavoided net
Of time still drawn in moment by moment.

Is there for such sorrow and love, Dowland, a tune
In your book? Heavy is it for lute to lift?
Yet we must make our poem of it and on the dune
Of this century scatter our sea-thrift.

Fable

They told us not to come this way at all
Or, if we must, to come early in the year
And to be through the town by afternoon
And to come many together
And to come armed.

But all the other ways were closed to us
By flood, fire, pestilence or bridges down
And it is October the last and late oclock
And we are alone
And arms we do not bear.

So it is with no surprise
That we see in the wicked alley
That opens like a fistula on the street
The ill-favoured group waiting,
Their hats pulled down over their eyes.

And beyond the town the country opens again
Cradled in late light, stilled with evening dew,
Untouched, uncompromised as though the world
    were new,
A vanishing and everlasting view.

The Beginners

How brave you are and all to learn,
The book so long, the discipline
So strict, the examiner so stern,
And when you have learned the sun goes in.

How young you are and all to go,
Uphill and down, the crooked and straight,
All the weather and all the woe,
The blowing darkness at the gate.

How good you are and that's the thing,
That is the iron, that is the bone,
The hammer will ring, the wind will sing,
The world will end before it is gone.

Sea-Captain

His eyes are cold blue daylight,
His face roughened and red;
Set on his bridge of shoulders
The wheelhouse of his head.

He walks the bucking coaster
Like a wheel set in a groove,
But lurches on the dry land
As though the earth did move.

Squints down at books and newsprint,
Things hard to understand,
But knows the vertical sky-wall
Like his own three-fingered hand.

And he makes no great matter
Of things so brave to me,
Bustle and muck of harbours,
Charge and recoil of the sea,

The cello winds and the calms,
The weather's stratagems,
And the solemn periodic
Lights with their famous names.

The Other Ghost

But there's another ghost who at cockcrow
Comes back from nowhere, takes me by the hand,
He loves no churchyards, does not mop and mow,
Would rather run than walk, would rather stand
Than sit down or lie low.

Why are we waiting? Off he goes, a rocket:
Ahead at once, he's out of sight soon after,
And no more seen that day. But when I chuck it
I hear asleep antipodean laughter,
And he will lap me on tomorrow's circuit.

Yet he's no brain, for all his sputnik flight:
Ask him a gambit, stratagem or counter,
How to outflank the enemy by night,
All he can say is, aim at the dead centre
And strike with all your might.

That he's a ghost I make no doubt at all:
Only a ghost could cut so clean through things,
Make gossamer impassable, stone wall
Pervious, and make his voice sound, when he sings,
Like telegraph wires did when I was small.

A Lullaby for the Newly Dead

Sleep away the years,
Sleep away the pain,
Wake, tomorrow,
A girl again.

Undo the proud journey
Mile upon mile,
Let the light bring only
A future and a smile.

Sleep away the loss,
Sleep away the gain,
Wake, tomorrow,
A girl again.

Sell back the knowledge
So dear bought
For the pennies of wonder
In a child's thought.

Sleep away the storm,
Sleep away the rain,
Wake, tomorrow,
A girl again.

Take up the forgotten
Running, dancing,
You are lighter now
Than a swift on the wing.

Let the world be a hero
And let the blood speak
For his coming with a pennon
In the lips, in the cheek.

Sleep away your loves,
The rose, the chain,
Wake, tomorrow,
A girl again.

Tomorrow

What do you see? A man in the half-light
And a child peering at something on a hill, and Oh
It's a fingerpost, says the child, but the man says No,
It's only a scarecrow; and they are both right.

There's a child busy at a game, and he has caught
Ptolemy in the wrong, for he felt the earth
Move; there's a man who has computed the worth
Of the solar system, and the answer is a nought.

What else do you see? There's a child watching the day
Break on the first word he ever spoke,
And the meaning rings in it; there's a man with a stroke
Who has laid all the words of his life away.

There's a child who has taken his first step and put
All the space of the astronomers in;
There's a man looking for himself and he has been
Round Asia for it and never budged a foot.

There is a child in a dark prison, and his
Eyes are looking for the sun, and that's a slim
Chance, or would be but the sun is looking for him.
There is also a man who has come to a precipice.

R. S. THOMAS

BORN in Cardiff, 1913. Educated at the University College
of North Wales at Bangor. A clergyman, who was Rector
of Manafon, Montgomeryshire, 1942–1954. Now Vicar of
Eglwys Fach, Machynlleth, Cardiganshire. Works: *The
Stones of the Field* (1946); *An Acre of Land* (1952); *Song at the
Year's Turning* (1955); *Poetry for Supper* (1958); *Tares*
(1961); *The Bread of Truth* (1963); *Pieta* (1966).

The pastor of a Welsh parish and interested in nature,
natural history, scenery, agriculture and the agricultural
worker, R. S. Thomas finds his themes round him. He is a
naturally reflective poet, and his subjects are the harsh, un-
feeling, Welsh hills and the farmers and labourers whom
these hills have made as harsh as themselves. The bleak
landscape and its tough, spiritually starved inhabitants both
have their dignity. The poet views them with compassion
and understanding, and judges them with dispassionate
sympathy. As Wordsworth saw Michael, he sees the Welsh
country people to have their own grandeur, hard-wrung
from the earth, beneath their drabness. Their small cir-
cumscribed world is a microcosm: birth and life and death
are everything here. Beneath the surface lie all the world's
passions—courage, hatred, love, and, above all, fortitude.
'He looks at men and nature in the light of eternity.' The

verse is as direct, firm and austere as the landscape. No word is wasted: the language is pared to the bone. Images are concrete and exact.

In *Evans*, there is an acute sense of desolation but it is not pessimistic. The bed is likened to a shore, and this faint association with departure opens the poem from its concentration on human wreckage and so gives it a wider scope.

No Through Road

All in vain. I will cease now
My long absorption with the plough,
With the tame and the wild creatures
And man united with the earth.
I have failed after many seasons
To bring truth to birth,
And nature's simple equations
In the mind's precincts do not apply.

But where to turn? Earth endures
After the passing, necessary shame
Of winter, and the old lie
Of green places beckons me still
From the new world, ugly and evil,
That men pry for in truth's name.

Death of a Poet

Laid now on his smooth bed
For the last time, watching dully
Through heavy eyelids the day's colour
Widow the sky, what can he say

Worthy of record, the books all open,
Pens ready, the faces, sad,
Waiting gravely for the tired lips
To move once—what can he say?

His tongue wrestles to force one word
Past the thick phlegm; no speech, no phrases
For the day's news, just the one word 'sorry';
Sorry for the lies, for the long failure
In the poet's war; that he preferred
The easier rhythms of the heart
To the mind's scansion; that now he dies
Intestate, having nothing to leave
But a few songs, cold as stones
In the thin hands that asked for bread.

A Welsh Testament

All right, I was Welsh. Does it matter?
I spoke the tongue that was passed on
To me in the place I happened to be,
A place huddled between grey walls
Of cloud for at least half the year.
My word for heaven was not yours.
The word for hell had a sharp edge
Put on it by the hand of the wind
Honing, honing with a shrill sound
Day and night. Nothing that Glyn Dŵr
Knew was armour against the rain's
Missiles. What was descent from him?

Even God had a Welsh name:
We spoke to him in the old language;
He was to have a peculiar care
For the Welsh people. History showed us
He was too big to be nailed to the wall
Of a stone chapel, yet still we crammed him
Between the boards of a black book.

Yet men sought us despite this.
My high cheek-bones, my length of skull
Drew them as to a rare portrait
By a dead master. I saw them stare
From their long cars, as I passed knee-deep
In ewes and wethers. I saw them stand
By the thorn hedges, watching me string
The far flocks on a shrill whistle.

And always there was their eyes' strong
Pressure on me; You are Welsh, they said;
Speak to us so; keep your fields free
Of the smell of petrol, the loud roar
Of hot tractors; we must have peace
And quietness.
           Is a museum
Peace? I asked. Am I the keeper
Of the heart's relics, blowing the dust
In my own eyes? I am a man;
I never wanted the drab rôle
Life assigned me, an actor playing
To the past's audience upon a stage
Of earth and stone; the absurd label
Of birth, of race hanging askew

About my shoulders. I was in prison
Until you came; your voice was a key
Turning in the enormous lock
Of hopelessness. Did the door open
To let me out or yourselves in?

Welsh Landscape

To live in Wales is to be conscious
At dusk of the spilled blood
That went to the making of the wild sky,
Dyeing the immaculate rivers
In all their courses.
It is to be aware,
Above the noisy tractor
And hum of the machine
Of strife in the strung woods,
Vibrant with sped arrows.
You cannot live in the present,
At least not in Wales.
There is the language for instance,
The soft consonants
Strange to the ear.
There are cries in the dark at night
As owls answer the moon,
And thick ambush of shadows,
Hushed at the fields' corners.
There is no present in Wales,
And no future;

There is only the past,
Brittle with relics,
Wind-bitten towers and castles
With sham ghosts;
Mouldering quarries and mines;
And an impotent people,
Sick with inbreeding,
Worrying the carcase of an old song.

The Hill Farmer Speaks

I am the farmer, stripped of love
And thought and grace by the land's hardness;
But what I am saying over the fields'
Desolate acres, rough with dew,
Is, Listen, listen, I am a man like you.

The wind goes over the hill pastures
Year after year, and the ewes starve,
Milkless, for want of the new grass.
And I starve, too, for something the spring
Can never foster in veins run dry.

The pig is a friend, the cattle's breath
Mingles with mine in the still lanes;
I wear it willingly like a cloak
To shelter me from your curious gaze.

The hens go in and out at the door
From sun to shadow, as stray thoughts pass
Over the floor of my wide skull.
The dirt is under my cracked nails;
The tale of my life is smirched with dung;
The phlegm rattles. But what I am saying
Over the grasses rough with dew
Is, Listen, listen, I am a man like you.

Affinity

Consider this man in the field beneath,
Gaitered with mud, lost in his own breath,
Without joy, without sorrow,
Without children, without wife,
Stumbling insensitively from furrow to furrow,
A vague somnambulist; but hold your tears,
For his name also is written in the Book of Life.

Ransack your brainbox, pull out the drawers
That rot in your heart's dust, and what have you to give
To enrich his spirit or the way he lives?
From the standpoint of education or caste or creed
Is there anything to show that your essential need
Is less than his, who has the world for church,
And stands bare-headed in the woods' wide porch
Morning and evening to hear God's choir
Scatter their praises? Don't be taken in
By stinking garments or an aimless grin;

He also is human, and the same small star,
That lights you homeward, has inflamed his mind
With the old hunger, born of his kind.

A Peasant

Iago Prytherch his name, though, be it allowed,
Just an ordinary man of the bald Welsh hills,
Who pens a few sheep in a gap of cloud.
Docking mangels, chipping the green skin
From the yellow bones with a half-witted grin
Of satisfaction, or churning the crude earth
To a stiff sea of clods that glint in the wind—
So are his days spent, his spittled mirth
Rarer than the sun that cracks the cheeks
Of the gaunt sky perhaps once in a week.
And then at night see him fixed in his chair
Motionless, except when he leans to gob in the fire.
There is something frightening in the vacancy of his mind.
His clothes, sour with years of sweat
And animal contact, shock the refined,
But affected, sense with their stark naturalness.
Yet this is your prototype, who, season by season
Against siege of rain and the wind's attrition,
Preserves his stock, an impregnable fortress
Not to be stormed even in death's confusion.
Remember him, then, for he, too, is a winner of wars,
Enduring like a tree under the curious stars.

An Old Man

Looking upon this tree with its quaint pretension
Of holding the earth, a leveret, in its claws,
Or marking the texture of its living bark,
A grey sea wrinkled by the winds of years,
I understand whence this man's body comes,
In veins and fibres, the bare boughs of bone,
The trellised thicket, where the heart, that robin,
Greets with a song the seasons of the blood.

But where in meadow or mountain shall I match
The individual accent of the speech
That is the ear's familiar? To what sun attribute
The honeyed warmness of his smile?
To which of the deciduous brood is german
The angel peeping from the latticed eye?

The Lonely Farmer

Poor hill farmer astray in the grass:
There came a movement and he looked up, but
All that he saw was the wind pass.
There was a sound of voices on the air,
But where, where? It was only the glib stream talking
Softly to itself. And once when he was walking

Along a lane in spring he was deceived
By a shrill whistle coming through the leaves:
Wait a minute, wait a minute—four swift notes;
He turned, and it was nothing, only a thrush
In the thorn bushes easing its throat.
He swore at himself for paying heed,
The poor hill farmer, so often again
Stopping, staring, listening, in vain,
His ear betrayed by the heart's need.

Evans

Evans? Yes, many a time
I came down his bare flight
Of stairs into the gaunt kitchen
With its wood fire, where crickets sang
Accompaniment to the black kettle's
Whine, and so into the cold
Dark to smother in the thick tide
Of night that drifted about the walls
Of his stark farm on the hill ridge.

It was not the dark filling my eyes
And mouth appalled me; not even the drip
Of rain like blood from the one tree
Weather-tortured. It was the dark
Silting the veins of that sick man
I left stranded upon the vast
And lonely shore of his bleak bed.

Enigma

A man is in the fields, let us look with his eyes,
As the first clouds ripen with the sunrise,
At the earth around us, marking the nameless flowers
That minister to him through the tedious hours
Of sweat and toil, their grave, half-human faces
Lifted in vain to greet him where he passes.
The wind ruffles the meadow, the tall clouds sail
Westward full-rigged, and darken with their shadow
The bright surface as a thought the mind.
The earth is beautiful, and he is blind
To it all, or notices only the weeds' way
Of wrestling with and choking the young hay
That pushes tentatively from the gaunt womb.
He cannot read the flower-printed book
Of nature, nor distinguish the small songs
The birds bring him, calling with wide bills,
Out of the leaves and over the bare hills;
The squealing curlew, and the loud thrush
Are both identical, just birds, birds;
He blames them sullenly as the agreed,
Ancestral enemies of the live seed,
Unwilling to be paid by the rich crop
Of music swelling thickly to the hedge top.

Blind? Yes, and deaf, and dumb, and the last irks most,
For could he speak, would not the glib tongue boast
A lore denied our neoteric sense,
Being handed down from the age of innocence?

Or would the cracked lips, parted at last, disclose
The embryonic thought that never grows?

The Country Clergy

I see them working in old rectories
By the sun's light, by candlelight,
Venerable men, their black cloth
A little dusty, a little green
With holy mildew. And yet their skulls,
Ripening over so many prayers,
Toppled into the same grave
With oafs and yokels. They left no books,
Memorial to their lonely thought
In grey parishes; rather they wrote
On men's hearts and in the minds
Of young children sublime words
Too soon forgotten. God in his time
Or out of time will correct this.

Chapel Deacon

Who put that crease in your soul,
Davies, ready this fine morning
For the staid chapel, where the Book's frown
Sobers the sunlight? Who taught you to pray

And scheme at once, your eyes turning
Skyward, while your swift mind weighs
Your heifer's chances in the next town's
Fair on Thursday? Are your heart's coals
Kindled for God, or is the burning
Of your lean cheeks because you sit
Too near that girl's smouldering gaze?
Tell me, Davies, for the faint breeze
From heaven freshens and I roll in it,
Who taught you your deft poise?

A Blackbird Singing

It seems wrong that out of this bird,
Black, bold, a suggestion of dark
Places about it, there yet should come
Such rich music, as though the notes'
Ore were changed to a rare metal
At one touch of that bright bill.

You have heard it often, alone at your desk
In a green April, your mind drawn
Away from its work by sweet disturbance
Of the mild evening outside your room.

A slow singer, but loading each phrase
With history's overtones, love, joy
And grief learned by his dark tribe
In other orchards and passed on
Instinctively as they are now,
But fresh always with new tears.

The View from the Window

Like a painting it is set before one,
But less brittle, ageless; these colours
Are renewed daily with variations
Of light and distance that no painter
Achieves or suggests. Then there is movement,
Change, as slowly the cloud bruises
Are healed by sunlight, or snow caps
A black mood; but gold at evening
To cheer the heart. All through history
The great brush has not rested,
Nor the paint dried; yet what eye,
Looking coolly, or, as we now,
Through the tears' lenses, ever saw
This work and it was not finished?

INDEX OF FIRST LINES